SRI AUROBINDO AND THE MOTHER

THE
SUPRAMENTAL TRANSFORMATION

First Edition 2011
Second Edition 2022
The Supramental Transformation
Loretta Shartsis

ISBN 978-93-95460-02-6 (print)
ISBN 978-93-95460-03-3 (ebook)

BISAC Code:
OCC000000 BODY, MIND & SPIRIT
HEA025000 HEALTH & FITNESS / Yoga
REL062000 Religion / Spirituality
REF019000, REFERENCE / Quotations

Thema Subject Category:
AKLB, Illustration
VX, Mind, body, spirit

Cataloging-in-Publication Data for this title is available from the Library of Congress.

Printed and bound in India by:
PRISMA, Aurelec/ Prayogshala,
Auroville 605101, Tamil Nadu, India

Digital Editions produced by:
DMI Systems Pvt Ltd, Vishnupuri,
Aligarh 202001, Uttar Pradesh, India

Published by PRISMA, an imprint of Digital Media Initiatives
www.prisma.haus, www.dmi.systems

Impressum

Acknowledgments: This book contains many of The Mother's reports on her own transformation, along with Sri Aurobindo's writings on the subject. The focus is on The Mother's experiences and the results, which she describes for us in detail.

We are all evolutionary beings, and, consciously or not, we receive something from the changes of consciousness in our subtle environment. There are now many people who are not only aware that great changes are taking place in the general consciousness, but who are also eager to receive the new consciousness and to participate in the change. This book gives an introduction and a comprehensive understanding of the supramental tranformation. It is a treasure-house of the new consciousness which, by its very nature, is accessible to anyone who reads with the aspiration to receive.

Quotation from Sri Aurobindo are protected by the copyright of the Sri Aurobindo Ashram Trust, Pondicherry. The text from the Mother's Agenda is protected by the copyright of the "Institut de Recherches Evolutives". Cover drawing © Loretta Shartsis, February 2011.

CONTENTS

INTRODUCTION

Sri Aurobindo and The Mother worked to make humanity and the earth ready for the future. A major aspect of this coming manifestation is a great change in the consciousness available to mankind. Today, man, at the summit of his evolution, is a mental being. Sri Aurobindo called this consciousness "Supramental" because man's next evolutionary step is to develop capacities beyond the mind.

Sri Aurobindo and The Mother saw that, as the new consciousness continues to manifest, this evolutionary process includes changes in man's physical body. They called the process "The Supramental Transformation". As part of her work here, The Mother, as the forerunner in this evolution, spent many years concentrating on the way to make it possible for her own physical body to receive this new consciousness. She left us many detailed descriptions of her realizations and experiences, and of the changes which occurred both in her consciousness and in her physical body.

This book contains many of The Mother's reports on her own transformation, along with Sri Aurobindo's writings on the subject. The focus is on The Mother's experiences and the results, which she describes for us in detail.

We are all evolutionary beings, and, consciously or not, we receive something from the changes of consciousness in our subtle environment. There are now many people who are not only aware that great changes are taking place in the general consciousness, but who are also eager to receive the new consciousness and to participate in the change. This book gives an introduction and a comprehensive understanding of the supramental tranformation. It is a treasure-house of the new consciousness which, by its very nature, is accessible to anyone who reads with the aspiration to receive.

The quotations are taken from a variety of sources. The quotations from Sri Aurobindo are identified by his symbol ⁂ placed above the text. Quotations from The Mother are identified by her symbol ⊛ placed above the text. References listing the sources can be found at the end of the book.

EVOLUTION

All is not finished in the unseen decree;
    A Mind beyond our mind demands our ken,
A life of unimagined harmony
    Awaits, concealed, the grasp of unborn men.

The crude beginnings of the lifeless earth,
    The mindless stirrings of the plant and tree
Prepared our thought; thought for a godlike birth
    Broadens the mould of our mortality.

A might no human will nor force can gain,
    A knowledge seated in eternity,
A bliss beyond our struggle and our pain
    Are the high pinnacles of our destiny.

O Thou who climb'dst to mind from the dull stone,
Face now the miracled summits still unwon.

Again the mighty yearning raised its flame
That asks a perfect life on earth for men
And prays for certainty in the uncertain mind
And shadowless bliss for suffering human hearts
And Truth embodied in an ignorant world
And godhead divinising mortal forms.

If man lives bound by his humanity,
If he is tied for ever to his pain,
Let a greater being then arise from man,
The superhuman with the Eternal mate
And the Immortal shine through earthly forms.
Else were creation vain and this great world
A nothing that in Time's moments seems to be.
But I have seen through the insentient mask;
I have felt a secret spirit stir in things
Carrying the body of the growing God:
It looks through veiling forms at veilless truth;
It pushes back the curtain of the gods;
It climbs towards its own eternity."

The earliest preoccupation of man in his awakened thoughts and, as it seems, his inevitable and ultimate preoccupation,—for it survives the longest periods of scepticism and returns after every banishment,—is also the highest which his thought can envisage. It manifests itself in the divination of Godhead, the impulse towards perfection, the search after pure Truth and unmixed Bliss, the sense of a secret immortality. The ancient dawns of human knowledge have left us their witness to this constant aspiration; today we see a humanity satiated but not satisfied by victorious analysis of the externalities of Nature preparing to return to its primeval longings. The earliest formula of Wisdom promises to be its last, —God, Light, Freedom, Immortality.

The progressive revelation of a great, a transcendent, a luminous Reality with the multitudinous relativities of this world that we see and those other worlds that we do not see as means and material, condition and field, this would seem then to be the meaning of the universe,—since meaning and aim it has and is neither a purposeless illusion nor a fortuitous accident.

What were earth's ages if the grey restraint
Were never broken and glories sprang not forth
Bursting their obscure seed, while man's slow life
Leaped hurried into sudden splendid paths
By divine words and human gods revealed?

We speak of the evolution of Life in Matter, the evolution of Mind in Matter; but evolution is a word which merely states the phenomenon without explaining it. For there seems to be no reason why Life should evolve out of material elements or Mind out of living form, unless we accept the Vedantic solution that Life is already involved in Matter and Mind in Life because in essenceMatter is a form of veiled Life, Life a form of veiled Consciousness. And then there seems to be little objection to a farther step in the series and the admission that mental consciousness may itself be only a form and a veil of higher states which are beyond Mind. In that case, the unconquerable impulse of man towards God, Light, Bliss, Freedom, Immortality presents itself in its right place in the chain as simply the imperative impulse by which Nature is seeking to evolve beyond Mind, and appears to be as natural, true and just as the impulse towards Life which she has planted in certain forms of Matter or the impulse towards Mind which she has planted in certain forms of Life.

If in the meaningless Void creation rose,
If from a bodiless Force Matter was born,
If Life could climb in the unconscious tree,
Its green delight break into emerald leaves
And its laughter of beauty blossom in the flower,
If sense could wake in tissue, nerve and cell
And Thought seize the grey matter of the brain,
And soul peep from its secrecy through the flesh,
How shall the nameless Light not leap on men,
And unknown powers emerge from Nature's sleep?

A life of unity, mutuality and harmony born of a deeper and wider truth of our being is the only truth of life that can successfully replace the imperfect mental constructions of the past which were a combination of association and regulated conflict, an accommodation of egos and interests grouped or dovetailed into each other to form a society, a consolidation by common general life-motives, a unification by need and the pressure of struggle with outside forces. It is such a change and such a reshaping of life for which humanity is blindly beginning to seek, now more and more with a sense that its very existence depends upon finding the way.

THE SUPRAMENTAL REALISATION

In order to know what the Supramental Realisation will be like, the first step, the first condition is to know what the supramental consciousness is. All those who have been, in one way or another, in contact with it have had some glimpse of the realisation to be. But those who have not, can yet aspire for that realisation, just as they can aspire to get the supramental knowledge. True knowledge means awareness by identity: once you get in touch with the supramental world, you can say something about its descent, but not before. What you can say before is that there will be a new creation upon earth; this you say through faith, since the exact character of it escapes you. And if you are called upon to define realisation, you may declare that, individually speaking, it means the transformation of your ordinary human consciousness into the divine and supramental. The consciousness is like a ladder: at each great epoch there has been one great being capable of adding one more step to the ladder and reaching a place where the ordinary consciousness had never been. It is possible to attain a high level and get completely out of the material consciousness; but then one does not retain the ladder, whereas the great achievement of the great epochs of the universe has been the capacity to add one more step to the ladder without losing contact with the material, the capacity to reach the Highest and at the same time connect the top with the bottom instead of letting a kind of emptiness cut off all connection between the different planes. To go up and down and join the top to the bottom is the whole secret of realisation, and that is the work of the Avatar. Each time he adds one more step to the ladder there is a new creation upon earth.... The step which is being added now Sri Aurobindo has called the Supramental; as a result of it, the consciousness will be able to enter the supramental world and yet retain its personal form, its individualisation and then come down to establish here a new creation. Certainly this is not the last, for there are farther ranges of being; but now we are at work to bring down the supramental, to effect a reorganisation of the world, to bring the world back to the true divine order. It is essentially a creation of order, a putting of everything in its true place; and the chief spirit or force, the Shakti active at present is Mahasaraswati, the Goddess of perfect organisation.

The work of achieving a continuity which permits one to go up and down and bring into the material what is above, is done inside the consciousness. He who is meant to do it, the Avatar, even if he were shut up in a prison and saw nobody and never moved out, still would he do the work, because it is a work in the consciousness, a work of connection between the Supermind and the material being. He does not need to be recognised, he need have no outward power in order to be able to establish this conscious connection. Once, however, the connection is made, it must have its effect in the outward world in the form of a new creation, beginning with a model town and ending with a perfect world.

To be or become something, to bring something into being is the whole labour of the force of Nature; to know, feel, do are subordinate energies that have a value because they help the being in its partial self-realisation to express what it is and help it too in its urge to express the still more not yet realised that it has to be.

To be and to be fully is Nature's aim in us; but to be fully is to be wholly conscious of one's being: unconsciousness, half consciousness or deficient consciousness is a state of being not in possession of itself; it is existence, but not fullness of being. To be aware wholly and integrally of oneself and of all the truth of one's being is the necessary condition of true possession of existence. This self-awareness is what is meant by spiritual knowledge: the essence of spiritual knowledge is an intrinsic self-existent consciousness; all its action of knowledge, indeed all its action of any kind, must be that consciousness formulating itself. All other knowledge is consciousness oblivious of itself and striving to return to its own awareness of itself and its contents; it is self-ignorance labouring to transform itself back into self-knowledge.

There are greater destinies mind cannot surmise
Fixed on the summit of the evolving Path
The Traveller now treads in the Ignorance,
Unaware of his next step, not knowing his goal.
Mind is not all his tireless climb can reach,
There is a fire on the apex of the worlds,
There is a house of the Eternal's light,
There is an infinite truth, an absolute power.
The Spirit's mightiness shall cast off its mask;
Its greatness shall be felt shaping the world's course:
It shall be seen in its own veilless beams,
A star rising from the Inconscient's night,
A sun climbing to Supernature's peak.
Abandoning the dubious middle Way,
A few shall glimpse the miraculous Origin
And some shall feel in you the secret Force
And they shall turn to meet a nameless tread,
Adventurers into a mightier Day.
Ascending out of the limiting breadths of mind,
They shall discover the world's huge design
And step into the Truth, the Right, the Vast.

The essential purpose and sign of the growing evolution here is the emergence of consciousness in an apparently inconscient universe, the growth of consciousness and with it growth of the light and power of the being; the development of the form and its functioning or its fitness to survive, although indispensable, is not the whole meaning or the central motive. The greater and greater awakening of consciousness and its climb to a higher and higher level and a wider extent of its vision and action is the condition of our progress towards that supreme and total perfection which is the aim of our existence. It is the condition also of the total perfection of the body. There are higher levels of the mind than any we now conceive and to these we must one day reach and rise beyond them to the heights of a greater, a spiritual existence. As we rise we have to open to them our lower members and fill these with those superior and supreme dynamisms of light and power; the body we have to make a more and more and even entirely conscious frame and instrument, a conscious sign and seal and power of the spirit. As it grows in this perfection, the force and extent of its dynamic action and its response and service to the spirit must increase; the control of the spirit over it also must grow and the plasticity of its functioning both in its developed and acquired parts of power and in its automatic responses down to those that are now purely organic and seem to be the movements of a mechanic inconscience. This cannot happen without a veritable transformation, and a transformation of the mind and life and very body is indeed the change to which our evolution is secretly moving and without this transformation the entire fullness of a divine life on earth cannot emerge. In this transformation the body itself can become an agent and a partner.

THE CALL OF THE IMPOSSIBLE

A godhead moves us to unrealised things.
    Asleep in the wide folds of destiny,
A world guarded by Silence' rustling wings
    Shelters their fine impossibility:

But parting quiver the caerulean gates;
    Strange splendours look into our dreaming eyes;
We bear proud deities and magnificent fates;
    Faces and hands come near from Paradise.

What shines above, waits darkling here in us:
    Bliss unattained our future's birthright is,
Beauty of our dim souls grows amorous,
    We are the heirs of infinite widenesses.

The impossible is our mask of things to be,
Mortal the door to immortality.

At present mankind is undergoing an evolutionary crisis in which is concealed a choice of its destiny; for a stage has been reached in which the human mind has achieved in certain directions an enormous development while in others it stands arrested and bewildered and can no longer find its way. A structure of the external life has been raised up by man's ever-active mind and life-will, a structure of an unmanageable hugeness and complexity, for the service of his mental, vital, physical claims and urges, a complex political, social, administrative, economic, cultural machinery, an organised collective means for his intellectual, sensational, aesthetic and material satisfaction. Man has created a system of civilisation which has become too big for his limited mental capacity and understanding and his still more limited spiritual and moral capacity to utilise and manage, a too dangerous servant of his blundering ego and its appetites. For no greater seeing mind, no intuitive soul of knowledge has yet come to his surface of consciousness which could make this basic fullness of life a condition for the free growth of something that exceeded it. This new fullness of the means of life might be, by its power for a release from the incessant unsatisfied stress of his economic and physical needs, an opportunity for the full pursuit of other and greater aims surpassing the material existence, for the discovery of a higher truth and good and beauty, for the discovery of a greater and diviner spirit which would intervene and use life for a higher perfection of the being: but it is being used instead for the multiplication of new wants and an aggressive expansion of the collective ego.

The Truth-Consciousness is everywhere present in the universe as an ordering self-knowledge by which the One manifests the harmonies of its infinite potential multiplicity. Without this ordering self-knowledge the manifestation would be merely a shifting chaos, precisely because the potentiality is infinite,— which by itself might lead only to a play of uncontrolled unbounded Chance.

In the workings of such a Truth-consciousness there would be a certain conscious seeing and willing automatism of the steps of its truth which would replace the infallible automatism of the inconscient or seemingly inconscient Force that has brought out of an apparent Void the miracle of an ordered universe, and this could create a new order of the manifestation of the Being in which a perfect perfection would become possible; even a supreme and total perfection would appear in the vistas of an ultimate possibility. If we could draw down this power into the material world, our agelong dreams of human perfectibility, individual perfection, the perfectibility of the race, of society, inner mastery over self and a complete mastery, governance and utilisation of the forces of Nature could see at long last a prospect of total achievement. This complete human self-fulfilment might well pass beyond limitations and be transformed into the character of a divine life. Matter after taking into itself and manifesting the power of life and the light of mind would draw down into it the superior or supreme power and light of the spirit and in an earthly body shed its parts of inconscience and become a perfectly conscious frame of the spirit. A secure completeness and stability of the health and strength of its physical tenement could be maintained by the will and force of this inhabitant; all the natural capacities of the physical frame, all powers of the physical consciousness would reach their utmost extension and be there at command and sure of their flawless action. As an instrument the body would acquire a fullness of capacity, a totality of fitness for all uses which the inhabitant would demand of it far beyond anything now possible. Even it could become a revealing vessel of a supreme beauty and bliss,—casting the beauty of the light of the spirit suffusing and radiating from it as a lamp reflects and diffuses the luminosity of its indwelling flame, carrying in itself the beatitude of the spirit, its joy of the seeing mind, its joy of life and spiritual happiness, the joy of Matter released into a spiritual consciousness and thrilled with a constant ecstasy. This would be the total perfection of the spiritualised body.

The supermind shall claim the world for Light
And thrill with love of God the enamoured heart
And place Light's crown on Nature's lifted head
And found Light's reign on her unshaking base.
A greater truth than earth's shall roof-in earth
And shed its sunlight on the roads of mind;
A power infallible shall lead the thought,
A seeing Puissance govern life and act,
In earthly hearts kindle the Immortal's fire.
A soul shall wake in the Inconscient's house;
The mind shall be God-vision's tabernacle,
The body intuition's instrument,
And life a channel for God's visible power.
All earth shall be the Spirit's manifest home,

A transformation of human nature can only be achieved when the substance of the being is so steeped in the spiritual principle that all its movements are a spontaneous dynamism and a harmonised process of the spirit. But even when the higher powers and their intensities enter into the substance of the Inconscience, they are met by this blind opposing Necessity and are subjected to this circumscribing and diminishing law of the nescient substance. It opposes them with its strong titles of an established and inexorable Law, meets always the claim of life with the law of death, the demand of Light with the need of a relief of shadow and a background of darkness, the sovereignty and freedom and dynamism of the spirit with its own force of adjustment by limitation, demarcation by incapacity, foundation of energy on the repose of an original Inertia. There is an occult truth behind its negations which only the Supermind with its reconciliation of contraries in the original Reality can take up and so discover the pragmatic solution of the enigma. Only the supramental Force can entirely overcome this difficulty of the fundamental Nescience; for with it enters an opposite and luminous imperative Necessity which underlies all things and is the original and final self-determining truth-force of the selfexistent Infinite.

All this might not come all at once, though such a sudden illumination might be possible if a divine Power and Light and Ananda could take their stand on the summit of our being and send down their force into the mind and life and body illumining and remoulding the cells, awaking consciousness in all the frame. But the way would be open and the consummation of all that is possible in the individual could progressively take place. The physical also would have its share in that consummation of the whole.

THE SILVER CALL

There is a godhead of unrealised things
    To which Time's splendid gains are hoarded dross;
A cry seems near, a rustle of silver wings
    Calling to heavenly joy by earthly loss.

All eye has seen and all the ear has heard
    Is a pale illusion by some greater voice
And mightier vision; no sweet sound or word,
    No passion of hues that make the heart rejoice

Can equal those diviner ecstasies.
    A Mind beyond our mind has sole the ken
Of those yet unimagined harmonies,
    The fate and privilege of unborn men.

As rain-thrashed mire the marvel of the rose,
Earth waits that distant marvel to disclose.

The divine life will give to those who enter into it and possess it an increasing and finally a complete possession of the truth consciousness and all that it carries in it; it will bring with it the realisation of the Divine in self and the Divine in Nature.

All that is sought by the God-seeker will be fulfilled in his spirit and in his life as he moves towards spiritual perfection. He will become aware of the transcendent reality, possess in the self-experience the supreme existence, consciousness, bliss, be one with Sachchidananda. He will become one with cosmic being and universal Nature: he will contain the world in himself, in his own cosmic consciousness and feel himself one with all beings; he will see himself in all and all in himself, become united and identified with the Self which has become all existences. He will perceive the beauty of the All-Beautiful and the miracle of the All-Wonderful; he will enter in the end into the bliss of the Brahman and live abidingly in it and for all this he will not need to shun existence or plunge into the annihilation of the spiritual Person in some self-extinguishing Nirvana. As in the Self, so in Nature, he can realise the Divine. The nature of the Divine is Light and Power and Bliss; he can feel the divine Light and Power and Bliss above him and descending into him, filling every strand of his nature, every cell and atom of his being, flooding his soul and mind and life and body, surrounding him like an illimitable sea and filling the world, suffusing all his feeling and sense and experience, making all his life truly and utterly divine.

I shall relate an experience of mine when I first met Sri Aurobindo in Pondicherry. I was in deep concentration, seeing things in the Supermind, things that were to be but which were somehow not manifesting. I told Sri Aurobindo what I had seen and asked him if they would manifest. He simply said, "Yes." And immediately I saw that the Supramental had touched the earth and was beginning to be realised! This was the first time I had witnessed the power to make real what is true: it is the very same power that will bring about the realisation in you of the truth when you come in all sincerity, saying, "This falsehood I want to get rid of", and the answer which you get is "Yes."

I saw the Omnipotent's flaming pioneers
Over the heavenly verge which turns towards life
Come crowding down the amber stairs of birth;
Forerunners of a divine multitude,
Out of the paths of the morning star they came
Into the little room of mortal life.
I saw them cross the twilight of an age,
The sun-eyed children of a marvellous dawn,
The great creators with wide brows of calm,
The massive barrier-breakers of the world
And wrestlers with destiny in her lists of will,
The labourers in the quarries of the gods,
The messengers of the Incommunicable,
The architects of immortality.
Into the fallen human sphere they came,
Faces that wore the Immortal's glory still,
Voices that communed still with the thoughts of God,
Bodies made beautiful by the spirit's light,
Carrying the magic word, the mystic fire,
Carrying the Dionysian cup of joy,
Approaching eyes of a diviner man,
Lips chanting an unknown anthem of the soul,
Feet echoing in the corridors of Time.
High priests of wisdom, sweetness, might and bliss,
Discoverers of beauty's sunlit ways
And swimmers of Love's laughing fiery floods
And dancers within rapture's golden doors,
Their tread one day shall change the suffering earth
And justify the light on Nature's face.

A manifestation of the Supermind and its truth-consciousness is then inevitable; it must happen in this world sooner or later. But it has two aspects, a descent from above, an ascent from below, a self-revelation of the Spirit, an evolution in Nature. The ascent is necessarily an effort, a working of Nature, an urge or nisus on her side to raise her lower parts by an evolutionary or revolutionary change, conversion or transformation into the divine reality and it may happen by a process and progress or by a rapid miracle. The descent or self-revelation of the Spirit is an act of the supreme Reality from above which makes the realisation possible and it can appear either as the divine aid which brings about the fulfilment of the progress and process or as the sanction of the miracle. Evolution, as we see it in this world, is a slow and difficult process and, indeed, needs usually ages to reach abiding results; but this is because it is in its nature an emergence from inconscient beginnings, a start from nescience and a working in the ignorance of natural beings by what seems to be an unconscious force. There can be, on the contrary, an evolution in the light and no longer in the darkness, in which the evolving being is a conscious participant and cooperator, and this is precisely what must take place here.

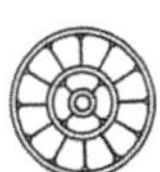

THE SUPRAMENTAL DESCENT

Do you know what the flower which we have called "Successful Future" signifies when given to you? It signifies the hope—nay, even the promise—that you will participate in the descent of the supramental world. For that descent will be the successful consummation of our work, a descent of which the full glory has not yet been or else the whole face of life would have been different. By slow degrees the Supramental is exerting its influence; now one part of the being and now another feels the embrace or the touch of its divinity; but when it comes down in all its self-existent power, a supreme radical change will seize the whole nature. We are moving nearer and nearer the hour of its complete triumph. Once the world-conditions are ready the full descent will take place carrying everything before it. Its presence will be unmistakable, its force will brook no resistance, doubts and difficulties will not torture you any longer. For the Divine will stand manifest—unveiled in its total perfection. I do not, however, mean to say that the whole world will at once feel its presence or be transformed; but I do mean that a part of humanity will know and participate in its descent—say, this little world of ours here. From there the transfiguring grace will most effectively radiate. And, fortunately for the aspirants, that successful future will materialise for them in spite of all the obstacles set in its way by unregenerate human nature!

DESCENT

All my cells thrill swept by a surge of splendour,
Soul and body stir with a mighty rapture,
Light and still more light like an ocean billows
    Over me, round me.

Rigid, stonelike, fixed like a hill or statue,
Vast my body feels and upbears the world's weight;
Dire the large descent of the Godhead enters
      Limbs that are mortal.

Voiceless, thronged, Infinity crowds upon me;
Presses down a glory of power eternal;
Mind and heart grow one with the cosmic wideness;
      Stilled are earth's murmurs.

Swiftly, swiftly crossing the golden spaces
Knowledge leaps, a torrent of rapid lightnings;
Thoughts that left the Ineffable's flaming mansions,
      Blaze in my spirit.

Slow the heart-beats' rhythm like a giant hammer's;
Missioned voices drive to me from God's doorway
Words that live not save upon Nature's summits,
      Ecstasy's chariots.

All the world is changed to a single oneness;
Souls undying, infinite forces, meeting,
Join in God-dance weaving a seamless Nature,
      Rhythm of the Deathless.

Mind and heart and body, one harp of being,
Cry that anthem, finding the notes eternal,—
Light and might and bliss and immortal wisdom
      Clasping for ever.

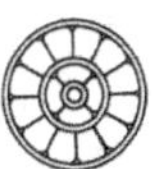

AUGUST 1954

When we speak of transformation, the meaning of
the word is still vague to us. It gives us the impression
of something that is going to happen which will set
everything right. The idea more or less boils down to this:

if we have difficulties, the difficulties will vanish; those who are ill will be cured of their illness; if the body has infirmities or incapacities, the infirmities or incapacities will fade away, and so forth ... But as I have said, it is very vague, it is only an impression. Now, what is quite remarkable about the body consciousness is that it is unable to know a thing with precision and in all its details except when it is just about to be realized. Thus, when the process of transformation becomes clear, when we are able to know by what sequence of movements and changes the total transformation will take place, in what order, by which path, as it were, which things will come first, which will follow – when everything is known, in all its details, it will be a sure indication that the hour of realization is near, for each time you perceive a detail accurately, it means that you are ready to carry it out.

In the meantime, one can have an overall view. For example, it is quite certain that under the influence of the supramental light, the transformation of the body consciousness will take place first then will come a progress in the mastery and control of all the movements and workings of all the body's organs; afterwards this mastery will gradually change into a kind of radical modification of the movement and then of the constitution of the organ itself. All this is certain, although rather vague to our perception. But what will finally take place – once the various organs are replaced by centers of concentration of forces, each with a different quality and nature and each acting according to its own special mode – is still a mere conception, and the body does not understand very well, for it is still very far from the realization, and the body can really understand only when it is on the point of being able to do.

I know there shall inform the inconscient cells,
At one with Nature and at height with heaven,
A spirit vast as the containing sky
And swept with ecstasy from invisible founts,
A god come down and greater by the fall.

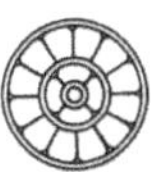

OCTOBER 17, 1957

One of the very first results of the supramental manifestation was to give the body a freedom and an autonomy it has never before known. And when I say freedom, I don't mean some psychological perception or an inner state of consciousness, but something else and far better – it is a new phenomenon in the body, in the cells of the body. For the first time, the cells themselves have felt that they are free, that they have the power to decide. When the new vibrations came and combined with the old ones, I felt it at once and it showed me that a new world was really taking birth.

In its normal state, the body always feels that it is not its own master: illnesses invade it without its really being able to resist them – a thousand factors impose themselves or exert pressure upon it. Its sole power is the power to defend itself, to react. Once the illness has got in, it can fight and overcome it – even modern medicine has acknowledged that the body is cured only when it decides to get cured; it is not the drugs per se that heal, for if the ailment is temporarily suppressed by a drug without the body's will, it grows up again elsewhere in some other form until the body itself has decided to be cured. But this implies only a defensive power, the power to react against an invading enemy – it is not true freedom.

But with the supramental manifestation, something new has taken place in the body: it feels it is its own master, autonomous, with its two feet solidly on the ground, as it were. This gives a physical impression of the whole being suddenly drawing itself up, with its head lifted high – I am my own master.

We live perennially with a burden on our shoulders, something that bows our heads down, and we feel pulled, led by all kinds of external forces, we don't know by whom or what, nor where to – this is what men call Fate, Destiny. When you do yoga, one of the first experiences – the experience of the kundalini, as it is called here in India – is precisely one in which the consciousness rises, breaks through this hard 'lid,' here, at the crown of the head, and at last you emerge into the Light. Then you see, you know, you decide and you realize – difficulties may still remain, but truly speaking one is above them. Well, as a result of the supramental manifestation, it is THIS experience that came into the body. The body straightened its head up and felt its freedom, its independence.

During the flu epidemic, for example, I spent every day in the midst of people who were germ carriers. And one day, I clearly felt that the body had decided not to catch this flu. It asserted its autonomy. You see, it was not a question of the higher Will deciding, no. It didn't take place in the highest consciousness: the body itself decided. When you are way above in your consciousness, you see things, you know things; but in actual fact, once you descend again into matter, it is like water running through sand. In this respect, things have changed, the body has a DIRECT power, independent of any outer intervention. Even though it is barely visible, I consider this to be a very important result.

And this new vibration in the body has allowed me to understand the mechanism of the transformation. It is not something that comes from a higher Will, not a higher consciousness that imposes itself upon the body: it is the body itself awakening in its cells, a freedom of the cells themselves, an absolutely new vibration that sets disorders right – even disorders that existed prior to the supramental manifestation.

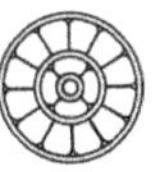

FEBRUARY 29, 1956

During the common meditation on Wednesday
This evening the Divine Presence, concrete and material, was there present amongst you. I had a form of living gold, bigger then the universe, and I was facing a huge and massive golden door which separated the world from the Divine.

As I looked at the door, I knew, and willed, in a single movement of consciousness, that "the time has come," and lifting with both hands a mighty golden hammer I struck one blow, one single blow on the door and the door was shattered to pieces.

Then the supramental Light and Force and Consciousness rushed down upon earth in an uninterrupted flow.

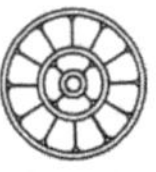

FEBRUARY 29, 1956

Lord, Thou hast willed, and I execute:
A new light breaks upon the earth,
A new world is born.
The things that were promised are fulfulled.

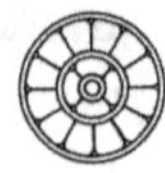

Mother reads Her report of the experience she had on February 3

Between the beings of the supramental world and men, almost the same separation exists as between men and animals. Some time ago I had the experience of identification with animal life, and it is a fact that animals do not understand us; their consciousness is so constructed that we elude them almost entirely.

And yet I have known pet animals—cats and dogs, but especially cats—that used to make an almost yogic effort of consciousness to reach us. But usually, when they see us as we live and act, they do not understand, they do not see us as we are and they suffer because of us. We are a constant enigma to them. Only a very tiny part of their consciousness has a link with us. And it is the same thing for us when we try to look at the supramental world. Only when the link of consciousness is established shall we see it—and even then only the part of our being which has undergone transformation in this way will be able to see it as it is—otherwise the two worlds would remain apart like the animal and human worlds.

The experience I had on the third of February is a proof of this. Before that I had had an individual subjective contact with the supramental world, whereas on the third of February I moved in it concretely, as concretely as I once used to walk in Paris, in a world that exists in itself, outside all subjectivity. It is like a bridge being thrown between the two worlds. Here is the experience as I dictated it immediately afterwards:

The supramental world exists permanently and I am there permanently in a supramental body. I had the proof of this even today when my earth-consciousness went there and remained there consciously between two and three o'clock in the afternoon.

Now, I know that what is lacking for the two worlds to unite in a constant and conscious relation, is an intermediate zone between the physical world as it is and the supramental world as it is. This zone remains to be built, both in the individual consciousness and the objective world, and it is being built. When I used to speak of the new world which is being created, it was of this intermediary zone that I was speaking. And similarly, when I am on this side, that is, in the field of the physical consciousness, and I see the supramental power, the supramental light and substance constantly penetrating matter, it is the construction of this zone which I see and in which I participate.

I was on a huge boat which was a symbolic representation of the place where this work is going on. This boat, as large as a city, is fully organised, and it had certainly already been functioning for some time, for its organisation was complete. It is the place where people who are destined for the supramental life are trained. These people—or at least a part of their being—had already undergone a supramental transformation, for the boat itself and everything on board was neither material nor subtle-physical nor vital nor mental—it was a supramental substance. This substance was of the most material supramental, the supramental substance which is closest to the physical world, the first to manifest. The light was a mixture of gold and red, forming a uniform substance of a luminous orange. Everything was like that—the light was like that, the people were like that—everything had that colour, although with various shades which made it possible to distinguish things from each other. The general impression was of a world without shadows; there were shades but no shadows. The atmosphere was full of joy, calm, order; everything went on regularly and in silence. And at the same time one could see all the details of an education, a training in all fields, by which the people on board were being prepared

This immense ship had just reached the shore of the supramental world and a first group of people who were destined to become the future inhabitants of this supramental world were to disembark. Everything had been arranged for this first landing. At the wharf several very tall beings were posted. They were not human beings, they had never been men before. Nor were they the permanent inhabitants of the supramental world. They had been delegated from above and posted there to control and supervise the landing. I was in charge of the whole thing from the beginning and all the time. I had prepared all the groups myself. I stood on the boat at the head of the gangway, calling the groups one by one and sending them down to the shore.

The tall beings who were posted there were inspecting, so to say, those who were landing, authorising those who were ready and sending back those who were not and who had to continue their training on board the ship. While I was there looking at everybody, the part of my consciousness which came from here became extremely interested; it wanted to see and recognise all the people, see how they had changed and check which ones were taken immediately and which ones had to remain to continue their training. After a while, as I stood there observing, I began to feel that I was being pulled back so that my body might wake up —a consciousness or a person here—and in my consciousness I protested, "No, no, not yet, not yet! I want to see the people!" I was seeing and noting everything with intense interest.... Things continued in this way until suddenly the clock here began to strike three, and this brought me back violently. There was a sensation of suddenly falling into my body. I came back with a shock because I had been called back very suddenly, but with all my memory. I remained quiet, without moving, until I could recollect the whole experience and keep it.

On the boat the nature of objects was not the one we know on earth; for instance, clothes were not made of cloth and what looked like cloth was not manufactured: it formed a part of the body, it was made of the same substance which took different forms. It had a kind of plasticity. When a change had to be made, it took place, not by any artificial and external means but by an inner operation, an operation of consciousness which gave form or appearance to the substance. Life created its own forms. There was one single substance in everything; it changed the quality of its vibration according to need and use.

Those who were sent back for fresh training were not of a uniform colour, it was as if their body had greyish, opaque patches of a substance resembling earthly substance; they were dull, as if they had not been entirely permeated with light, not transformed. They were not like that everywhere, only in places. The tall beings on the shore were not of the same colour, at least they did not have that orange tint; they were paler, more transparent. Except for one part of their body, one could only see the outline of their form. They were very tall, they seemed not to have any bones and could take any form according to their need. Only from the waist down had they a permanent density, which was not perceptible in the rest of their body. Their colour was much lighter, with very little red, it was more golden or even white. The parts of whitish light were translucent; they were not positively transparent but less dense, more subtle than the orange substance.

When I was called back and while I was saying "Not yet", each time I had a brief glimpse of myself, that is, of my form in the supramental world. I was a mixture of the tall beings and the beings aboard the ship. My upper part, particularly the head, was only a silhouette whose contents were white with an orange fringe. Going down towards the feet, the colour became more like that of the people on the boat, that is, orange; going upwards, it was more translucent and white and the red grew less. The head was only a silhouette with a sun shining within it; rays of light came from it which were the action of the will.

As for the people I saw on board the ship, I recognised them all. Some were from here, from the Ashram, some came from elsewhere, but I know them too. I saw everybody but as I knew that I would not remember them all when I returned, I decided not to give any names. Besides, it is not necessary. Three or four faces were very clearly visible, and when I saw them, I understood the feeling I had here on earth when looking into their eyes: there was such an extraordinary joy.... People were mostly young, there were very few children and they were about fourteen or fifteen, certainly not below ten or twelve—I did not remain long enough to see all the details. There weren't any very old people, apart from a few exceptions. Most of the people who went ashore were middle-aged, except a few. Already, before this experience, some individual cases had been examined several times at a place where people capable of being supramentalised were examined; I had a few surprises and noted them; I even told some people about it. But the ones whom I put ashore today, I saw very distinctly; they were middle-aged, neither young children nor old people, apart from a few rare exceptions, and that corresponded fairly well with what I expected. I decided not to say anything, not to give any names. As I did not remain until the end, it was not possible for me to get an exact picture; the picture was not absolutely clear or complete. I do not want to say things to some and not to others.

What I can say is that the point of view, the judgment, was based exclusively on the substance of which the people were made, that is, whether they belonged completely to the supramental world, whether they were made of that very special substance. The standpoint taken is neither moral nor psychological.

It is probable that the substance their bodies were made of was the result of an inner law or inner movement which at that time was not in question. At least it is quite clear that the values are different. When I came back, simultaneously with the recollection of the experience I knew that the supramental world is permanent, that my presence there is permanent, and that only a missing link was necessary for the connection to be made in the consciousness and the substance, and it is this link which is now being forged. I had the impression—an impression which remained for quite a long time, almost a whole day—of an extreme relativity—no, not exactly that: the impression that the relation between this world and the other completely changed the standpoint from which things should be evaluated or appraised. This standpoint had nothing mental about it and it gave a strange inner feeling that lots of things we consider good or bad are not really so. It was very clear that everything depended on the capacity of things, on their aptitude in expressing the supramental world or being in relation with it. It was so completely different, sometimes even altogether contrary to our ordinary appraisal. I recollect one little thing which we usually consider to be bad; how strange it was to see that in truth it was something excellent! And other things we consider to be important have in fact absolutely no importance at all: whether a thing is like this or like that is not at all important. What is very obvious is that our appraisal of what is divine or undivine is not right. I even laughed to see certain things.... Our usual feeling of what is antidivine seems artificial, seems based on something that's not true, not living—besides, what we call life here did not seem living to me compared with that world—anyway, this feeling should be founded on our relation between the two worlds and on how things make the relation between them easier or more difficult.

This would make a great difference in our appraisal of what brings us nearer to the Divine or what separates us from Him. In people too I saw that what helps them to become supramental or hinders them from it, is very different from what our usual moral notions imagine. I felt how... ridiculous we are.

JANUARY 10, 1961

Love, in its essence and in its origin, is like a white flame obliterating ALL resistances. You can have the experience yourself: whatever the difficulty in your being, whatever the weight of accumulated mistakes, the ignorance, incapacity, bad will, a single SECOND of this Love – pure, essential, supreme – melts everything in its almighty flame. One single moment and an entire past can vanish. One single TOUCH of That in its essence and the whole burden is consumed.

It's easy to understand how someone who has this experience can spread it and act upon others, since to have it you must touch the unique, supreme Essence of the whole manifestation – the Origin and the Essence, the

Source and the Reality of all that is; then you immediately enter the realm of Unity where there is no more separation among individuals: it's a single vibration that can repeat itself endlessly in outer forms.

If you go high enough, you come to the Heart of everything. Whatever manifests in this Heart can manifest in all things. This is the great secret, the secret of divine incarnation in an individual form. For in the normal course of things, what manifests at the center is only realized in the outer form with the awakening and RESPONSE Of the will within the individual form. But if the central Will is constantly, permanently represented in one individual, he can then serve as an intermediary between that Will and all beings, and will FOR THEM. Whatever this being perceives and consciously offers to the supreme Will is replied to as if it came from each individual being. And if individuals happen to be in a more or less conscious and voluntary relationship with this representative being, their relationship increases his efficacy and the supreme Action can work in Matter in a much more concrete and permanent way. This is the reason for these descents of what could be called 'polarized' consciousnesses that always come to earth for a particular realization, with a definite purpose and mission – a mission decided upon before the actual embodiment. These mark the great stages of the supreme incarnations upon earth.

And when the day comes for the manifestation of supreme Love – a crystalized, concentrated descent of supreme Love – that will truly be the hour of Transformation, for nothing will be able to resist That.

But as it's all-powerful, a certain receptivity must be prepared on earth so its effects are not devastating. Sri Aurobindo has explained it in one of his letters. Someone asked him, 'Why doesn't this Love come now?', and he replied something like this: If divine Love in its essence were to manifest on earth, it would be like an explosion; for the earth is not supple enough or receptive enough to widen to the measure of this Love. The earth must not only open itself but become wide and supple. Matter – not just physical Matter, but the substance of the physical consciousness as well – is still much too rigid.

BLISS OF IDENTITY

All Nature is taught in radiant ways to move,
    All beings are in myself embraced.
O fiery boundless Heart of joy and love,
    How art thou beating in a mortal's breast!

It is Thy rapture flaming through my nerves
    And all my cells and atoms thrill with Thee;
My body Thy vessel is and only serves
    As a living wine-cup of Thy ecstasy.

I am a centre of Thy golden light
    And I its vast and vague circumference;
Thou art my soul great, luminous and white
    And Thine my mind and will and glowing sense.

Thy spirit's infinite breath I feel in me;
My life is a throb of Thy eternity.

NOVEMBER 5, 1961

About the discovery of the Supermind in the Veda and by Sri Aurobindo. There is something I don't quite grasp.

Because in the Veda it's incomplete.

No, they had a *hint*, like a vision of the 'thing,' but there is no proof that they realized it. What's more, had they realized it, it seems to me that we would certainly have found some traces – but no traces remain.

Theon knew something about it, and he called it 'the new world' or 'the new creation on earth and the glorified body' (I don't remember his exact terminology); but he knew of the Supermind's existence – it had been revealed to him and he announced its coming. He said it would be reached THROUGH the discovery of the God within. And for him, … this meant a greater density – which seems to be a correct experience. Well, on my side, I have made investigations and had innumerable visions concerning the earth's history, and I spoke about it a good deal with Sri Aurobindo....

(silence)

According to what Sri Aurobindo saw and what I saw as well, the Rishis had the contact, the experience – how to put it? … A kind of lived knowledge of the thing, coming like a promise, saying, 'THAT is what will be.' But it's not permanent. There's a big difference between their experience and the DESCENT – what Sri Aurobindo calls 'the descent of the Supermind': something that comes and establishes itself.

Even when I had that experience [the 'first supramental manifestation' of February 29, 1956], when the Lord said, 'The time has come,' well, it was not a complete descent; it was the descent of the Consciousness, the Light, and a part, an aspect of the Power. It was immediately absorbed and swallowed up by the world of Inconscience, and from that moment on it began to work in the atmosphere. But it was not THE thing that comes and gets permanently established; when that happens, we won't need to speak of it – it will be obvious!

Although the experience of '56 was one more forward step, it's not.... It's not final.

And what the Rishis had was a sort of promise – an INDIVIDUAL experience.

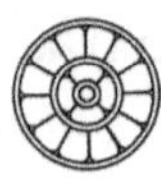

JANUARY 12, 1962

(Mother refers to her experience February 1958 when her consciousness went to the link that was forming between the Supramental world and our world.)

The people on that ship had these two capacities: one, the capacity for indefinite expansion of consciousness on all planes, including the material; and two, limitless plasticity in order to follow the movement of the Becoming.

It was taking place in the subtle physical. The people who had patches on their bodies and had to be sent back were always the ones who lacked the plasticity those two movements required. But the main thing was the movement of expansion; the progressive movement, the movement of following the Becoming, seemed to be a subsequent preoccupation – for those who had landed. The preparation on the boat concerned that capacity for expansion.

Another thing I didn't mention to you when I related the experience was that the ship had no engine. Everything was set in motion through will power – people, things (even the clothes people wore were a result of their will). And this gave all things and every person's shape a great suppleness, because there was an awareness of this will – which is not a mental will but a will of the Self, what could be called a spiritual will or a soul-will (to give the word soul that particular meaning). I have that experience right here when there's an absolute spontaneity in action, I mean when the action – for instance, an utterance or a movement – is not determined by the mind, and not even (not to mention thought or intellect), not even by the mind that usually sets us in motion. Generally, when

we do something, we can perceive in ourselves a will
to do it; when you watch yourself, you see this: there is
always (it can happen in a flash) the will to do. When
you are conscious and watch yourself doing something,
you see in yourself the will to do it – this is where the
mind intervenes, its normal intervention, the established
order in which things happen. But the supramental action
is decided by a leap over the mind. The action is direct,
with no need to go through the mind. Something enters
directly into contact with the vital centers and activates
them without going through the mind – yet in full
consciousness. The consciousness doesn't function in the
usual sequence, it functions from the center of spiritual
will straight to matter.

And so long as you can keep that absolute immobility
in the mind, the inspiration is absolutely pure – it comes
pure. When you can catch and hold onto this while you're
speaking, then what comes to you is unmixed too, it stays
pure.

This is an extremely delicate functioning, probably
because we're not used to it – the slightest movement, the
slightest mental vibration disrupts everything. But as long
as it lasts, it's perfectly pure. And in a supramentalized
life this has to be the CONSTANT state. Mentalized will
should no longer intervene; because you may well have a
spiritual will, your life may be the constant expression of
spiritual will (it's what happens to all who feel themselves
guided by the Divine within), but it still comes through
a mental transcription. Well, as long as it's that way, it's
not the supramental life. The supramental life NO LONGER
goes through the mind – the mind is an immobile zone
of transmission. The least little twitch is enough to upset
everything.

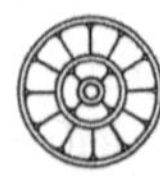

(After a perilous month, Mother has suddenly had the formidable, decisive experience, and she gives her first message. She is lying on her bed in the room upstairs, and has become quite thin. It is around ten in the morning. Her voice has greatly changed. Schoolchildren can be heard playing in the distance.)

Night of April 12-13.

Suddenly in the night I woke up with the full awareness of what we could call the Yoga of the world. The Supreme Love was manifesting through big pulsations, and each pulsation was bringing the world further in its manifestation. It was the formidable pulsations of the eternal, stupendous Love, only Love: each pulsation of the Love was carrying the universe further in its manifestation.

And the certitude that what is to be done is done and the Supramental Manifestation is realized.

Everything was Personal, nothing was individual.

This was going on and on and on and on....

The certitude that what is to be done is DONE.

All the results of the Falsehood had disappeared: Death was an illusion, Sickness was an illusion, Ignorance was an illusion – something that had no reality, no existence.... Only Love, and Love, and Love, and Love – immense, formidable, stupendous, carrying everything.

And how, how to express in the world? It was like an impossibility, because of the contradiction.... But then it came: "You have accepted that this world should know the Supramental Truth ... and it will be expressed totally, integrally." Yes, yes....

And the thing is DONE.

(long silence)

The individual consciousness came back, just the sense of a limitation, limitation of pain; without that, no individual.

And we set off again on the way, certain of the Victory.

The heavens are ringing with chants of Victory!

Truth alone exists; Truth alone shall manifest. Onward! ... Onward!

Gloire à Toi, Seigneur, Triomphateur suprême!

(silence)

And now, to work.

Patience ... endurance ... perfect equanimity. And absolute faith.

(silence)

Compared to the experience, whatever I say is nothing, nothing, nothing but words.

And our consciousness is the same, absolutely the same as the Lord's. There was no difference, no difference at all....

We are That, we are That, we are That.

(silence)

Later on, I will explain it more clearly. The instrument is not yet ready.

It is only the beginning.

* * *

Mother later added:

The experience lasted at least four hours. There are many things I will speak of later.

Then suddenly there came a downward look.
As if a sea exploring its own depths,
A living Oneness widened at its core
And joined him to unnumbered multitudes.
A Bliss, a Light, a Power, a flame-white Love
Caught all into a sole immense embrace;
Existence found its truth on Oneness' breast
And each became the self and space of all.
The great world-rhythms were heart-beats of one Soul,
To feel was a flame-discovery of God,
All mind was a single harp of many strings,
All life a song of many meeting lives;
For worlds were many, but the Self was one.
This knowledge now was made a cosmos' seed:
This seed was cased in the safety of the Light,
It needed not a sheath of Ignorance.
Then from the trance of that tremendous clasp
And from the throbbings of that single Heart
And from the naked Spirit's victory
A new and marvellous creation rose.
Incalculable outflowing infinitudes
Laughing out an unmeasured happiness
Lived their innumerable unity;
Worlds where the being is unbound and wide
Bodied unthinkably the egoless Self;
Rapture of beatific energies
Joined Time to the Timeless, poles of a single joy;
White vasts were seen where all is wrapped in all.
There were no contraries, no sundered parts,
All by spiritual links were joined to all
And bound indissolubly to the One:
Each was unique, but took all lives as his own,
And, following out these tones of the Infinite,
Recognised in himself the universe.

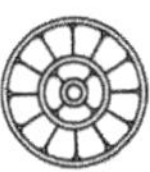

MAY 13, 1962

(This is the first conversation with Mother in two months. She is still reclining on her chaise longue. She looks quite pale and fragile, almost translucent. She enlarges upon the experience she had a month earlier, on April 13. The following text was not taped but noted down from memory and then read out to Mother.)

I was at the Origin – I WAS the Origin. For more than two hours, consciously, here on this bed, I was the Origin. And it was like gusts – like great gusts ending in explosions. And each one of these gusts was a span of the universe.

It was Love in its supreme essence – which has nothing to do with what people normally understand by that word.

And each gust of this essence of Love was dividing and spreading out ... but they weren't forces, it was far beyond the realm of forces. The universe as we know it no longer existed; it was a sort of bizarre illusion, bearing no relation to THAT. There was only the truth of the universe, with those great gusts of color – they were colored – great gusts colored with something that is the essence of color.

It was stupendous. I lived more than two hours like that, consciously.

And then a Voice was explaining everything to me (not exactly a Voice, but something that was Sri Aurobindo's origin, like the most recent gust from the Origin). As the experience unfolded, this Voice explained each gust to me, each span of the universe; and then it explained how it all became like this *(Mother makes a gesture of reversal):* the distortion of the universe. And I was wondering how it was possible, with that Consciousness, that supreme Consciousness, to relate to the present, distorted universe. How to make the connection without losing that

Consciousness? A relationship between the two seemed impossible. And that's when that sort of Voice reminded me of my promise, that I had promised to do the Work on earth and it would be done. "I promised to do the Work and it will be done."

Then began the process of descent, and the Voice was explaining it to me – I lived through it all in detail, and it wasn't pleasant. It took an hour and a half to change from that true Consciousness to the individual consciousness. Because throughout the experience this present individuality no longer existed, this body no longer existed, there were no more limits, I was no longer here – what was here was THE PERSON. An hour and a half was needed to return to the body-consciousness (not the physical consciousness but the body-consciousness), to the individual body-consciousness.

The first sign of the return to individuality was a prick of pain, a tiny point *(Mother holds between her fingers a minuscule point in the space of her being)*. Yes, because I have a sore, a sore in a rather awkward place, and it hurts *(Mother laughs)*. So I felt the pain: it was the sign of individuality coming back. Other than that, there was nothing any more – no body, no individual, no limits. But it's strange, I have made a strange discovery: I used to think it was the individual *(Mother touches her body)* who experienced pain and disabilities and all the misfortunes of human life; well, I perceived that what experiences misfortunes is not the individual not my body, but that each misfortune, each pain, each disability has its own individuality as it were, and each one represents a battle.

And my body is a world of battles.
It is the battlefield.

$$* \ ^* \ *$$

(When this text was read to Mother, she gave the following modification.)

I would prefer a word other than "descent," because there was no sensation or notion of descent – none at all.... It could be called the process of materialization or individualization – "transformation of consciousness" would be more exact. It is the process of changing from the true Consciousness to the distorted consciousness – that's it exactly.

You say it yourself: the transition from the true Consciousness to ordinary consciousness.

That's it exactly. "Descent" doesn't convey the actual sensation – there was no sensation of descent. None. Neither of ascent nor descent. None at all. Those creative gusts had no POSITION in relation to the creation; it was.... There was ONLY THAT. THAT ALONE existed. Nothing else.

And everything happened within That.

Really, it was.... There was neither high nor low nor within nor without – none of those existed any more. There was only THAT.

It was ... "something" expressing itself, manifesting itself through these gusts. Something that was EVERYTHING. There was nothing else, there was really nothing but THAT. So to speak of high, low, descent won't do at all.

If you like, we could put "the process of return"....

Of return to the body-consciousness. Or of materialization.

It is because of the spiritual Person, the Divinity in the individual, that perfection or liberation—salvation, as it is called in the West—has to be individual and not collective; for whatever perfection of the collectivity is to be sought after, can come only by the perfection of the individuals who constitute it. It is because the individual is That, that to find himself is his great necessity. In his complete surrender and self-giving to the Supreme it is he who finds his perfect self-finding in a perfect self-offering. In the abolition of the mental, vital, physical ego, even of the spiritual ego, it is the formless and limitless Individual that has the peace and joy of its escape into its own infinity. In the experience that he is nothing and no one, or everything and everyone, or the One which is beyond all things and absolute, it is the Brahman in the individual that effectuates this stupendous merger or this marvellous joining, Yoga, of its eternal unit of being with its vast all-comprehending or supreme all-transcending unity of eternal existence. To get beyond the ego is imperative, but one cannot get beyond the self—except by finding it supremely, universally. For the self is not the ego; it is one with the All and the One and in finding it it is the All and the One that we discover in our self: the contradiction, the separation disappears, but the self, the spiritual reality remains, united with the One and the All by that delivering disappearance.

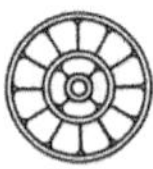

MAY 15, 1962

(Satprem reads to Mother his notes from the May 13 conversation and asks for further details on the April 13 experience:)

About that promise you received....

I didn't receive a promise – this Voice made me remember a promise I had made. I was saying to myself, "How to connect this true Consciousness to the other one – it's impossible! " And just then I seemed to hear ... not Sri Aurobindo exactly, because then you immediately think of a particular body, but that sort of Voice saying to me, "Your promise. You said you would do the Work." So that's when I said, "Yes, I shall do the Work." And from that moment on the process of materialization began, the entire transition from the true Consciousness to the ordinary consciousness.

I didn't receive a promise, but a reminder of the promise I had made.

And was that what allowed you to say, "The thing is done"?

No – it was the experience.
The experience. When.... I haven't told you this part.

(long silence)

When I was those gusts, those gusts of Love.... When I was conscious of the last one, the one organized outwardly, as it were, by Sri Aurobindo – materializing as the avatar Sri Aurobindo – then came the absolute certainty that the thing was done, that it was decreed.

And the moment I became aware that it was decreed, I thought, "But how can THAT be translated into that? How can the two be joined?" That was when the words came: "You promised to do it, therefore you will do it"; and slowly the transition began, as if I were again being sent back to do it. Yes, as if ... "You promised to do it and you will do it"; well, that's what I meant by a promise. And I came back towards this body to do it.

I said [on April 3] the body was the battlefield, that the battle was being waged IN this body. And then in that experience [of April 13] I was sent back into the body, because the thing – that last creative gust – had to be realized through this body.

...The physical consciousness is something very complex; it includes the whole physical, conscious world.

But are you making a distinction between the body-consciousness and the physical consciousness?...

My physical consciousness has been universalized for a long, long time, it encompasses all terrestrial movements; but the body is limited solely to this small concentration of substance *(Mother touches her body)* – that's what I call the body-consciousness.

And when I said, "I have left the body," it certainly didn't mean I have left the physical consciousness – my overall contact with the terrestrial world has remained the same. It concerns only the purely bodily aspect, the specific concretization or concentration of substance giving each of us a different body – a different APPEARANCE.

And a rather illusory appearance, besides. As soon as you rise to a certain height (I saw it quite clearly during that progressive reconcretization), this appearance quickly loses its reality. Our external appearance is very, very illusory. Our particular form (this one's form, that one's form), the form we see with our physical eyes is very superficial, you know. From the vital world onwards, it's completely different.

Well.... I think that's all I can say for today.

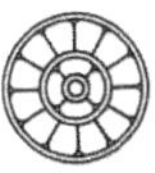

The boon that we have asked from the Supreme is the greatest that the Earth can ask from the Highest, the change that is most difficult to realise, the most exacting in its conditions. It is nothing less than the descent of the supreme Truth and Power into Matter, the supramental established in the material plane and consciousness and the material world and an integral transformation down to the very principle of Matter. Only a supreme Grace can effect this miracle.

The supreme Power has descended into the most material consciousness but it has stood there behind the density of the physical veil, demanding before manifestation, before its great open workings can begin, that the conditions of the supreme Grace shall be there, real and effective.

A total surrender, an exclusive self-opening to the divine influence, a constant and integral choice of the Truth and rejection of the falsehood, these are the only conditions made. But these must be fulfilled entirely, without reserve, without any evasion or presence, simply and sincerely down to the most physical consciousness and its workings.

This would mean an entry or approach into what might be called a truth-consciousness self-existent in which the being would be aware of its own realities and would have the inherent power to manifest them in a Time-creation in which all would be Truth following out its own unerring steps and combining its own harmonies; every thought and will and feeling and act would be spontaneously right, inspired or intuitive, moving by the light of Truth and therefore perfect. All would express inherent realities of the spirit; some fullness of the power of the spirit would be there. One would have overpassed the present limitations of mind: mind would become a seeing of the light of Truth, will a force and power of the Truth, Life a progressive fulfilment of the Truth, the body itself a conscious vessel of the Truth and part of the means of its self-effectuation and a form of its self-aware existence.

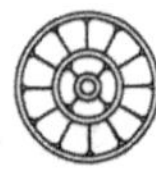

MARCH 7, 1964

I noticed (I've known it for some time, but it was quite concrete this time) that in my rest, as soon as I am at rest, the body is completely identified with the material substance of the earth, that is to say, the experience of the material substance of the earth becomes its own – which may be expressed by all sorts of things (it depends on the day, on the occasion). I had known for a long time that it was no longer the individual consciousness; it isn't the collective consciousness of mankind: it's a terrestrial consciousness, meaning it also contains the material substance of the earth, including the unconscious substance. Because I have prayed a lot, concentrated a lot, aspired a lot for the transformation of the Inconscient (since it is the essential condition for the "thing" to happen) – because of that there has been a kind of identification.

Last night it became a certainty.

And something began to descend – not "descend": to manifest and permeate; permeate and fill this terrestrial consciousness. What a force it had! What a power! ... I had never felt that kind of intensity in the material world. A stability, a power! Everything in the sense of a power, everything in the sense of a thrust forward – a thrust forward: progress, evolution, transformation. Everything like that. As if everything, everything were filled with a power of transformation – not "transformation," not transmutation, I don't know how to explain it.... Not the final transformation that will change the appearance, not that: it was the ananda of progress. The ananda of progress, like the ananda of progress of the animal becoming man, of man becoming superman – it wasn't transformation, it wasn't what will respond to that progress: it was progress. And with a plenitude, a constancy, and No RESISTANCE ANYWHERE: there was no panic anywhere, no resistance anywhere; everything was enthusiastically participating.

It lasted more than an hour.

APRIL 10, 1965

I have been asked a question *(Mother looks for a note)*:

How can I love the Lord? I have never seen Him and never He speaks to me.

This is my answer:

It is not what one sees or hears that one loves, it is love that one loves through the forms and sounds, and of all love the most perfect love, the most loving love is the Lord's love.

When I wrote it, it was an extraordinarily intense experience: one cannot love anything but love, and it is love that one loves behind all things – it is love that one loves. It is Love that loves itself everywhere.

MAY 19, 1965

In the Manifestation, perfection is to have a movement of transformation or unfolding identical to the divine Movement, the essential Movement. Whereas all that belongs to the unconscious or tamasic creation tries to keep its existence unchanged, instead of lasting by constant transformation.

...

From a practical standpoint, that's obvious.

But everyone takes his stand.... I have all the examples here, I have a little selection of samples of all the attitudes, and I see the reactions very clearly. I see the same Force – the same single Force – acting in this selection of samples and, of course, producing different effects; but those "different" effects are, to the deep vision, very superficial: it's just "they like to think that way, so then they like to think that way." But to tell the truth, the inner advance, the inner development, and the essential vibration aren't affected – not in the least. One aspires with all his heart to Nirvana, the other aspires with all his will to the supramental manifestation, and in both cases the vibratory result is about the same. And it's a whole mass of vibrations which prepares itself more and more to ... to receive what must be.

JUNE 18, 1965

[Mother speaks about one of her experiences at night when she met Sri Aurobindo in the subtle world.]

Last night, at one point we prepared a certain number of things that were at the same time like food, medicine, and a way to transform Matter. It had different colors, it was in test tubes, and he explained it all to me. But that wasn't the first time: it has happened very often. But then, the best part of it is that when I wake up, all the precise details are immediately swept away! I seem to feel a hand that comes and takes it all away – on purpose.

But I remember, I still have the image in which he is demonstrating things with his test tubes. There was a man ... who looked like a scientist (a man about forty years old, between forty and fifty, young but not very young) and very thoughtful-looking. He was sitting. I don't know what his nationality was, I don't remember, but he was modern; he was modern, with modern clothes, and Sri Aurobindo showed him his test tubes with things in them and the effect on a totality of matter. I was there, looking on (I was looking with great interest), and I understood everything then. And I still see the image, but the mental knowledge, the mental translation that would have enabled me to say, "Now I know," prrt! taken away. It's the same thing every time.

Which means it must be given to people other than me for them to use it, because they have a brain better prepared than mine, and better conditions of research.

It's clear that the work is getting done.

AUGUST 21, 1965

Since the 15th, there has been a whole work of preparation for the transformation .... What could I call it? ... A transfer of power.

The cells, the whole material consciousness, used to obey the inner individual consciousness – the psychic consciousness most of the time, or the mental (but the mind had been silent for a long time). But now this material mind is organizing itself like the other one, or the other ones, rather, like the mind of all the states of being – do you know, it is educating itself. It is learning things and organizing the ordinary science of the material world. When I write, for instance, I have noticed that it takes great care not to make spelling errors; and it doesn't know, so it inquires, it learns, it looks up in the dictionary or it asks. That's very interesting. It wants to know. You see, all the memory that came from mental knowledge went away a long, long time ago, and I used to receive indications only like this (*gesture from above*). But now it's a sort of memory being built from below, and with the care of a little child who educates himself but who wants to know, who doesn't want to make errors – who is perfectly conscious of his ignorance, and who wants to know. And the truly interesting thing is that it knows this knowledge to be quite ... more than relative, simply conventional, but it is like an instrument that would like to be free of defects, like a machine that would like to be perfect.

It is a rather recent awakening. There has been a sort of reversal of consciousness.

And at night it corresponds to thoroughly strange activities: a completely new way of seeing, feeling and observing people and things. Last night, for example, for over two hours there was a clear vision – an active vision (through action, that is) – of the way in which human consciousnesses make the most simple things complicated and difficult. It was fantastic – fantastic. And then, this consciousness was spontaneously impelled by the divine Presence, but it followed the others' human movements with the clear perception of the simple thing and of the way in which it becomes complicated. It was symbolic, with images; an activity in images in the sense that it wasn't purely material, physical as we know it here, but in a symbolic, imaged physical (in which the material world is seen as clay). It was very interesting.

Only, there was a very great intensity of transformation, and (how can I explain?) ... It's like a shift in the directing will. And then, there was materially, physically, a sort of surprise, and a need to identify with the new direction – it's a little difficult. It's difficult to explain, too.... It's no longer the same thing that makes you act – "act" or anything, of course: move, walk, anything. It isn't the same center any longer. And then if, by habit, you try to reconnect with the old center, oh, that creates a great disorder, and you must be very careful not to let habit, the old habit, express itself and manifest.

It's hard to express it. It is still too much just an action.

This morning, for example, several times for a certain length of time (I don't know how long, but not a very short time: a quarter of an hour, half an hour, I don't know), the body's cells, that is, the body's form had the experience that staying together or dissolving depends on a certain attitude – an attitude or a will; something that has to do with will and attitude. And with the perception (sometimes simultaneously an almost double perception, one being more a memory and the other a lived thing) of what makes you move, act, know; the old way like a memory, and the new way in which, obviously, there is no reason at all to dissolve, except if you choose to do so – it's meaningless, it's something meaningless: why dissolve?

The Supermind is in its very essence a truth-consciousness, a consciousness always free from the Ignorance which is the foundation of our present natural or evolutionary existence and from which nature in us is trying to arrive at self-knowledge and world-knowledge and a right consciousness and the right use of our existence in the universe. The Supermind, because it is a truth-consciousness, has this knowledge inherent in it and this power of true existence; its course is straight and can go direct to its aim, its field is wide and can even be made illimitable. This is because its very nature is knowledge: it has not to acquire knowledge but possesses it in its own right; its steps are not from nescience or ignorance into some imperfect light, but from truth to greater truth, from right perception to deeper perception, from intuition to intuition, from illumination to utter and boundless luminousness, from growing widenesses to the utter vasts and to very infinitude.

...

As its knowledge is always true, so too its will is always true; it does not fumble in its handling of things or stumble in its paces. In the Supermind feeling and emotion do not depart from their truth, make no slips or mistakes, do not swerve from the right and the real, cannot misuse beauty and delight or twist away from a divine rectitude. In the Supermind sense cannot mislead or deviate into the grossnesses which are here its natural imperfections and the cause of reproach, distrust and misuse by our ignorance.

Even an incomplete statement made by the Supermind is a truth leading to a further truth, its incomplete action a step towards completeness. All the life and action and leading of the Supermind is guarded in its very nature from the falsehoods and uncertainties that are our lot; it moves in safety towards its perfection.

AUGUST 28, 1965

(Regarding the conversation of August 21 and the experience of the "transfer of power" to the cellular consciousness:)

I said the other day that this aggregate of cells had changed its initiating power. It struck me as a unique experience, as something that had never occurred before. Unfortunately, it didn't last long. But the experience has left a kind of certitude in the body: it is less uncertain about the future. As if the experience came to tell the body, "This is how things will be."

If it stays on, it clearly means immortality.

I remember, when I told that experience, it was no longer something personal at all: if you can catch that....

SEPTEMBER 30, 1966

In all the transition from plant to animal and from animal to man (especially from animal to man), the differences of form are, ultimately, minor: the true transformation is the intervention of another agent of consciousness. All the differences between the life of the animal and the life of man stem from the intervention of the Mind; but the substance is essentially the same and it obeys the same laws of formation and construction. There isn't much difference, for instance, between the calf being formed in a cow's womb and the child being formed in its mother's womb. There is one difference: that of the Mind's intervention. But if we envisage a PHYSICAL being, that is, as visible as the physical now is and with the same density, for instance a body that wouldn't need blood circulation and bones (especially these two things: the skeleton and

53

blood circulation) ... it's very hard to imagine. And as long as it is like this, with this blood circulation, this functioning of the heart, we could imagine – we can imagine – the renewal of strength, of energy through a power of the Spirit, through other means than food. It's conceivable. But the rigidity, the solidity of the body, how is it possible without a skeleton?... So it would be an infinitely greater transformation than that from animal to man; it would be a transition from man to a being that would no longer be built in the same way, that would no longer function in the same way, that would be like a densification or concretization of ... "something." Up till now, it doesn't correspond to anything we have seen physically, unless the scientists have found something I am not aware of.

We may conceive of a new light or force giving the cells a sort of spontaneous life, a spontaneous strength.

Yes, that's what I said: food can disappear. That's conceivable.

But the whole body could be driven by that force. The body could remain supple, for instance. While still having its bone structure, it could remain supple, with the suppleness of a child.

But that's just why a child can't stand! He can't exert himself. What would replace the bone structure, for example?

The same elements could be there, but endowed with suppleness. Elements whose firmness doesn't stem from hardness but from the force of light, no?

Yes, that's possible.... Only, what I mean is that it may again take place through a large number of new creations. Will the transition from man to this being, for instance, perhaps take place through all kinds of other intermediaries? You understand, what I find formidable is the switch from one to the other.

I can very well conceive of a being who could, through spiritual power, the power of his inner being, absorb the necessary forces, renew himself and remain ever young; that's quite easily conceivable; even providing for a certain suppleness so as to be able to change the form if necessary. But the complete disappearance of this system of construction right away – from one to the other right away, that seems ... It appears to require stages.

Obviously, unless something happens (which we are forced to call a "miracle" because we can't understand how it could happen), how can a body like ours become a body entirely built and driven by a higher force, and without a material support? ... How can this (Mother pinches the skin of her hands), how can this change into that other thing?... It appears impossible.

It seems miraculous, but ...

Yes, in all my experiences, I understand quite well the possibility of not having to eat anymore, of that whole process being done away with (changing the method of absorption, for instance, is possible), but how do you change the structure?

It doesn't seem impossible to me.

It doesn't?

No, maybe it's imagination, but I can readily imagine a spiritual power entering the body and producing a sort of luminous inflation, and everything suddenly blossoms out like a flower. This body, which is crumpled in on itself, blossoms out, becomes radiant, supple, luminous.

Supple and plastic, we can also conceive it could be plastic, that is, the form wouldn't be fixed as it is now. All that is conceivable, but ...

But I can very well see it as a sort of luminous blossoming: the Light must have that force. And it doesn't destroy anything in the present structure.

But visible, that can be touched?

Yes. It's simply like a blossoming. What's closed up blossoms out like a flower, that's all; but it's still the flower's structure, only it's in full bloom and radiant. No?

Yes, but ... *(Mother shakes her head and remains silent for a while).* I lack experience, I don't know.

I am absolutely convinced (because I've had experiences that proved it to me) that the life of this body – its life, what makes it move and change – can be replaced by a force; that is to say, a sort of immortality can be created, and the wear and tear can disappear. These two things are possible: the power of life can come, and the wear and tear can disappear. And it can come about psychologically, through total obedience to the divine Impulsion, so that every moment you have the force you need, you do the thing that must be done – all these things, all of them are certitudes. Certitudes. They're not a hope, not an imagining: they are certitudes. Of course, you must educate the body and slowly transform and change the habits. It can be done, all that can be done. But the question is, how much time would it take to do away with the necessity (to take just this problem) of the skeleton? This is still very far ahead, it seems to me. Which means many intermediary stages will be needed. Sri Aurobindo said that life can be prolonged indefinitely. Yes, that's clear. But we aren't yet built with something that completely escapes dissolution, the necessity of dissolution. Bones are very durable, they can even last a thousand years if conditions are favorable, that's agreed, but it doesn't mean immortality IN PRINCIPLE. Do you understand what I mean?

No. Do you think it would have to be a nonphysical substance?

I don't know if it's nonphysical, but it's a physical I am unaware of! And it's not substance as we now know it, and especially not the construction we now know.

I don't know, but if it has to be a PHYSICAL body (as Sri Aurobindo said it would), it seemed to me (but that may be a daydream) that it could be like a lotus bud, for example: our present body is like a small, closed, hard lotus bud, and ... it blossoms out, it becomes a flower.

Yes, but that, mon petit, it's ...

Is there anything this Light can't do with the elements it has?? The materials remain the same, the elements remain the same, but transfigured.

But vegetal things aren't immortal.

No, it's only a comparison.

Well, that's just the point!

There's only this question: I can conceive of a perpetual change; I could even conceive of a flower that doesn't wither; but it's this principle of immortality.... Which means, basically, a life that escapes the necessity of renewal: the eternal Force would manifest directly and eternally, and this would still be a physical body (*Mother touches the skin of her hands*).

I quite understand a progressive change and that this substance could be made into something capable of renewing itself eternally from within outward. That would be immortality. But it seems to me that between what is now, what we are, and that other mode of life, a lot of stages might be necessary. You see, if for instance you ask these cells, with all the consciousness and experience they now have, "Is there something you cannot do?", in their sincerity they will answer, "No, what the Lord wills, I can do." That's their state of consciousness. But the appearance is otherwise. The personal experience is like this: all that I do with the Lord's Presence, I do effortlessly, without difficulty, without fatigue, without wear and tear, like that (Mother spreads out her arms in a great, harmonious Rhythm), but it's still open to the whole influence from outside and the body is forced to do things that aren't directly the expression of the supreme Impulsion, hence the fatigue, the friction.... So a supramental body suspended in a world that's not the earth is not the thing!

No.

Something is needed that has the power to resist the contagion. Man cannot resist the contagion from the animal, he can't, he has constant relationships. Well, how will that being manage? ... It would seem that for a long time – a long time – he will still be subject to the laws of contagion.

I don't know, it doesn't seem impossible to me.

No?

It seems to me that that Power of Light being here, what can affect it?

But the whole world would disappear! That's the problem, you understand.

When That comes, when the Lord is there, there isn't one in a thousand for whom it's not terrifying. And not to the reason, not to the thought: to the flesh, like that. So assume – assume it happens and a being is the condensation and expression, an embodiment of the supreme Power, of the supreme Light – what would happen?!

Well, that's the whole problem.

Yes.

Because I don't see the difficulty of the transformation in itself. It rather seems to be the difficulty of the world.

If everything could be transformed at the same time, it would be all right, but it's clearly not like that. If one being were transformed all alone ...

Yes, perhaps it would be unbearable.

Indeed!

Maybe that's the whole problem.

Multiply a thousand times what very small children feel. (I am talking about those who are exclusively physical, human beings, not those who are reincarnations.) When they are purely physical beings, they can't approach me, mon petit! They start crying and trembling! Yet I love them and welcome them with all my tenderness and as much calm as possible – they start trembling and then get frightened, it's too strong. With those who carry something else in themselves, the reincarnations, it's different: they open out, they are happy; but when there's nothing but this, that is, the external substance ... I've seen adults come (I did the experiment: I charge the atmosphere, the Lord is present), well, I've seen forty-year-old men enter that and ... brrt! literally run away, disregarding all social courtesy, and after having ASKED to come, you understand! Anyway everything was there to allow them to behave decently – impossible, they couldn't.

But even in my case, having the experience of you, knowing you well, at times it's fearsome.

Ah, you see.

It's not frightening, but ... it's really ... fearsome.

I am not putting words into your mouth!

Of course one knows – inside one knows there's nothing to fear, but still ...

Yes.

No, it's the substance that fears.
There.
So take the consciousness of a very small child, when you yourself ...

In your eyes, there is at times ... there is something ...

(Mother laughs)

OCTOBER 26, 1966

Sri Aurobindo wrote somewhere, I don't remember in what connection, that in a certain state of consciousness one had the power to CHANGE THE PAST. I found that very striking.

Because it's an experience I've had several times, and with all this work I am doing now, I understand better. You see, what seems to be perpetuated or preserved isn't individuals: it's states of consciousness – states of consciousness. Those states of consciousness manifest through many individuals and many different lives, and those states of consciousness are what progress towards a more and more luminous perfection. There are now, at present, all kinds of "categories" of states of consciousness that come one upon another in order to be put in contact with the Truth, the Light, the perfect Consciousness, and at the same time they have retained a sort of imprint (like a memory) of the moments when they manifested.

There is a big work of transformation of the material states of consciousness going on: the states of consciousness nearest to the Inconscient, the most material states of consciousness. They come like that [to present themselves to Mother], with one or two examples of their previous manifestation (perhaps even their first emergence from the Inconscient), and then I see the transition (along with what has transformed them, changed them or even simply altered them through successive manifestations), the transition up to the point when they are now presented before the supreme Consciousness for the final transformation. This is a perpetual work, so to speak, because, interestingly, it's a work I can go on doing while seeing people. Generally my work was interrupted when I saw people, because I was busy with them and that diminished and limited the work: they represented a small aggregate of difficulties that enormously shrank the Action [of Mother]. But now it's no longer like that. And the interesting point is that it places people in this or that "curve of transformation" of the consciousness. For some time I have been seeing a considerable number of people I had never seen before (with all the old or familiar people there was no difficulty, but with the new ones it generally caused a shrinking of the work), and now with this "study" of states of consciousness, people are placed: here, there, here *(Mother draws different levels in space)*. And if they are receptive, they must go away [after seeing Mother] with a new impulse to transform themselves. Those who aren't receptive just miss it; but they are no longer a disturbance: they come in and go out. And from that I know what state they are in – I can even do it with photos, but when I see people it's much more complete. Photos are no more than one moment of their being, while here, even what isn't being manifested is there, hidden behind, and can be seen, so I see the person more completely. It's very interesting. It transforms this whole burden of visitors into something interesting.

THE HIDDEN PLAN

However long Night's hour, I will not dream
    That the small ego and the person's mask
Are all that God reveals in our life-scheme,
    The last result of Nature's cosmic task.

A greater Presence in her bosom works;
    Long it prepares its far epiphany:
Even in the stone and beast the godhead lurks,
    A bright Persona of eternity.

It shall burst out from the limit traced by Mind
    And make a witness of the prescient heart;
It shall reveal even in this inert blind
    Nature, long veiled in each inconscient part,

Fulfilling the occult magnificent plan,
The world-wide and immortal spirit in man.

JANUARY 21, 1967

Something rather indefinable as yet is happening.

The body was in the habit of fulfilling its functions automatically, as something natural, which means that for it, the question of their importance or usefulness did not arise: it didn't have that mental, for instance, or vital vision of things, of what's "important" or "interesting" and what isn't. That didn't exist. But now that the cells are growing conscious, they seem to stand back *(gesture)*: they look at themselves, they begin to watch themselves act, and they very much wonder, "What's the use of all this?" And then, an aspiration: "How, how should things truly be? What's our purpose, our usefulness, our basis? Yes, what should our basis and our 'standard' of life be?" To put it mentally again, we might say, "How will we be when we are divine? What will be the difference? What's the divine way of being?" And what speaks there is that whole kind of physical base entirely made up of thousands of small things absolutely indifferent in themselves, whose raison d'être lies only in their totality, like a support to another action, but which in themselves seem devoid of any meaning. And then, it's again the same thing: a sort of receptivity, of silent opening to let oneself be permeated, and a very subtle perception of a way of being that might be luminous, harmonious.

That way of being is still quite indefinable; but in this seeking there is a constant perception (which translates as a vision) of a multicolored light, with all the colors – all the colors not in layers but as though *(stippling gesture)* combined in dots, a combination of all the colors. Two years ago (a little more than two years, I forget), when I met the Tantrics, when I came into contact with them, I started seeing that light, and I thought it was the "Tantric light," the Tantric way of seeing the material world. But now I see it constantly, associated with everything, and it seems to be what we might call a "perception of true Matter." All possible colors are combined without being mixed together *(same stippling gesture)*, and combined in luminous dots. Everything is as though made up of this. And it seems to be the true mode of being – I am not yet sure, but at any rate it's a far more conscious mode of being.

I see it all the time: with eyes open, eyes closed, all the time. It gives a strange perception (with regard to the body), a strange perception at the same time of subtlety, permeability (if I may call it that), of suppleness of form, and not exactly a removal but a considerable lessening of the rigidity of forms (the rigidity is removed, not the forms: a suppleness in the forms). As for the body, the first times it felt that in some part or the other, it felt ... when it happens it's a bit lost, with the sense of something eluding it. But if one remains very quiet and waits quietly, it's simply replaced by a sort of plasticity and fluidity that seems to be a new mode of the cells.

It might probably be what, on the material level, must take the place of the physical ego; that is to say, it seems the rigidity of the form must give place to this new way of being. Of course, the first contact is always very ... surprising. But the body is getting used to it little by little. What's a little difficult is the moment of transition from one way to the other. It's done very progressively, yet at the moment of transition there are a few seconds that are ... the least we can say is "unexpected."

JULY 12, 1967

I remember, when I came back after having BEEN those bursts – those pulsations, those bursts of creative Love, when I returned to the ordinary consciousness (while retaining the very real memory of That, of the state), well, that state, which I felt to be pulsations of creative Love, is what must, is That which must replace here this consciousness of concrete reality – which is, which becomes unreal: it's like something lifeless – hard, dry, inert, lifeless. And to our ordinary consciousness (I remember how it was in the past), that's what gives you the impression, "This is concrete, this is real." Well, "this," this sensation, is what must be replaced by the phenomenon of consciousness of that Pulsation. And That (*Mother makes an intense gesture enfolding her whole face)* is at the same time all-light, all-power, all-intensity of love, and such FULLNESS! It's so full that ... where That is, nothing else can exist. And when That is here, in the body, in the cells, then all you have to do is focus It on someone or something, and order is instantly restored in the person or the thing.

So, translated into ordinary words, it "heals." It heals the disease. But it doesn't heal it: it annuls it.... Yes, it annuls it.

It unrealizes it.

Absolutely. I have concrete proof of it.
Any disease, any disease whatsoever.

(silence)

And the condition of all the cells (the vibrations that make up this body) is undeniably what makes the thing [healing] possible or not; that is, depending on the body's condition, it serves either as a transmitter, or on the contrary as an obstruction. Because it's not a "higher force" acting in others THROUGH Matter: it's a direct action *(horizontal gesture, on a level)* from matter to matter.

What people generally call "healing power" is a very great mental or vital power that imposes itself through the resistance of Matter – but this isn't at all the same thing! It's the contagion of a vibration. And then it's irrevocable.

But it's gone in a flash. It's only a promise or an example of what will be: it WILL be like that, obviously. Obviously. When? ... That's another question.

(silence)

Right here, this Vibration is felt as ... *(Mother gestures as if everything were swelling)*. You understand, it [the body's ordinary condition] is tied up, it's tied and bound, I might almost say hardened, I don't know; and at such times, it seems to swell, to expand.

Only, it's momentary.

65

SEPTEMBER 30, 1967

Did you feel anything special?... Because the last two or three days, but especially last night and this morning, it was the body learning, the cells learning ... I told you that the work till now has been the change – the transfer – from acting out of habit and reaction to letting the divine Consciousness act. And this morning, for a part of the night and the whole morning until people started coming, with every action, every movement, every gesture, all the tiny little things (when, for instance, a problem is put by someone or a decision has to be made, for years the answer has been coming from above), but now with all material movements, also the inner movements, with the attitude of the body, of the cells, the absolutely material consciousness, with everything, everything – the old method was gone.

It began with the perception of the remaining difference between how things were and how they should be, then that perception disappeared and there only remained "that".... Something (how can I explain?) ... The English word smooth is the most expressive; everything is done *smoothly*, everything without exception: getting washed, brushing one's teeth, washing one's face, everything (as regards eating, for a long time that has been worked on in order that it should be done in the true way). It always begins with *(Mother opens her hands)* this sort of *surrender* (I don't know the right word, it's neither abdication nor offering but between the two; I don't know, there is no French word for it), the surrender of the WAY in which we do things: not of the thing in itself, which is quite unimportant (in that state there is no "big" and "small," no "important" and "unimportant"). And it's something so ... *(vast, even gesture)* uniform in its simplicity, there is nothing

that clashes or grates or causes difficulties anymore or ...
(all those words express things so crudely): it's something
that moves forward on and on so ... *(same vast, even gesture)*
the nearest word is *smoothly*, that is, without resistance. I
don't know. And it's not an intensity of delight, it's not
that: that also is so even, so regular *(same vast gesture)*, but
not uniform: it's innumerable. And EVERYTHING is like that
(same gesture), in a single ... rhythm (the word "rhythm" is
violent). It's not a uniformity, but something so even, and
which feels so sweet, you know, and with a TREMENDOUS
power in the smallest things.

NOVEMBER 22, 1967

(Mother takes flowers) I'll put them in water.... Flowers
are the beauty of life.

And there is a progress.

Oh?

At the end of the physical demonstration [on December
2], all the children will pray in chorus, and the prayer has
been written by me. I will read it to you.

But I hadn't thought about it: they asked me for it, and
I wrote it.

They must have read the Bulletin, and then they asked
me for a prayer – a prayer that would really be the body's.
I answered:

THE PRAYER OF THE CELLS IN THE BODY

Now that by the effect of the Grace we are slowly
emerging out of inconscience and waking up to a
conscious life, an ardent prayer rises in us for more
light, more consciousness:

"O Supreme Lord of the Universe, we implore Thee, give us the strength and the beauty, the harmonious perfection needed to be Thy divine instruments upon earth."

It's almost a proclamation.

There. So we'll put it into French.

They will say it after their demonstration; it seems they are going to show the whole evolution of physical culture, and then, at the end, they will say, "We have not reached the end, we are at the beginning of something, and here is our prayer."

I was very glad.

You said there is a progress?

A progress! It's a tremendous progress! The thought had never occurred to them, never; taken as a whole, they had never thought of the transformation: their thought was to become the best athletes in the world and all the usual nonsense.

The body, you see, they've asked for a prayer of the BODY. They have finally understood that the body must begin to transform itself into something else. Previously, they were all full of the whole history of physical culture in every country, in which country it's most developed, the use of the body as it is, and ... and so on. Anyway, it was the Olympic ideal. Now, they have leaped beyond: that is the past, now they want the transformation.

You understand, people were asking to be divine in their mind and vital – that is, the whole ancient history of spirituality, the same old theme for centuries – but now, it's the BODY. It's the body that asks to participate. It's certainly a progress.

Yes, but one can see how in the mind the aspiration sustains itself, how it lives by itself. In the heart too, one can see how

*the aspiration lives. But in the body? How can one awaken that
aspiration in the body?*

But good God! it's fully awakened! It's been for months
in me! So it means they've felt it, they are feeling it.

How it's done? – It's being done.

But how can one in oneself ...

No, no, no. If it has been done in one body, it can be
done in all bodies.

Yes, but I ask how.... Yes, how?

Well, that's what I have been trying to explain for
months.

It's, first of all, awakening the consciousness in the
cells....

Well, yes!

Yes, but once it's done it's done: the consciousness keeps
awakening more and more, the cells live consciously,
aspire consciously. I have been trying to explain it, good
Lord, for months! For months I have been trying to explain
it. And so, that's just what pleased me: it's that they have
at least understood the possibility of it.

The same consciousness which was the vital's and the
mind's monopoly has become corporeal: the consciousness
acts in the body's cells.

The body's cells grow into something conscious,
entirely conscious.

A consciousness which is independent, absolutely
independent of the vital consciousness or the mental
consciousness: it's a corporeal consciousness.

(silence)

And this physical mind, which Sri Aurobindo said was
an impossibility and something going round in circles
which would do so forever, without consciousness,

precisely, like a sort of machine, this physical mind has been converted, it has fallen silent, and in silence it has received inspiration from the Consciousness. And it has started praying again: the same prayers that were earlier in the mind.

I quite understand all that can take place in you, but...

But since it's taking place in one body, it can take place in all bodies! I am not made of anything different from others. The difference is the consciousness, that's all. It's made of exactly the same thing, with the same elements, I eat the same things, and it was made in just the same way.

And it was as dull, as dark, as unconscious, as stubborn as all other bodies in the world.

It began when the doctors declared I was seriously ill, that was the beginning. Because the entire body was emptied of its habits and forces, and then, slowly, slowly, the cells woke up to a new receptivity and opened directly to the divine Influence.

Every cell is vibrating.

Otherwise, it would be hopeless! If this matter, which began as ... Even a stone is already an organization; it was certainly worse than a stone: the inert, absolute Inconscient. Then, little by little, little by little, it awakens. One can see it, you know, one sees it: one just has to open one's eyes to see it. Well, the same thing is now taking place: for the animal to become a man, it didn't take anything else than the infusion of a consciousness – a mental consciousness – and now, it's the awakening of that consciousness which was there, deep down, in the very depths. The mind has withdrawn, the vital has withdrawn, everything has withdrawn; when I was supposedly ill, the mind had gone away, the vital had gone away, and the body was left to itself – purposely. And that's why, it's precisely because the vital and mind had gone that it looked like a very serious illness. And then, in the body left to itself, the cells little by little started awakening to the consciousness (gesture of a rising aspiration); once those two had gone, the consciousness which had been infused into the body THROUGH the vital (from the mind to the vital and from the vital to the body) started slowly, slowly emerging. It began with that burst of Love from all the way up, from the extreme, supreme altitude; then, little by little, little by little, it came down to the body. Then that sort of physical mind, that is, something totally and completely idiotic going round and round in circles, forever repeating the same thing over and over again, cleared up little by little and grew conscious, organized, then fell silent. And then in that silence, the aspiration expressed itself in prayers.

(silence)

It's a denial of all the spiritual assertions of the past: "If you want to live fully conscious of the divine life, leave your body – the body cannot follow." Well, Sri Aurobindo came and said, "Not only can the body follow, but it can be the base that will manifest the Divine."

The work remains to be done.

But now there is a certitude. The result is still very far – very far ahead, there is much to do before the crust, the outermost surface experience as it is, can manifest what takes place within (not "within" in the spiritual depths: within in the body). For it to be able to manifest what is within ... That will come last, which is very good because if it came earlier, we would neglect the work; we would be so happy that we'd forget to complete the work. Everything must have been done within, everything must be fully and thoroughly changed, then the outside will express it.

But it's all ONE SINGLE substance, the very same everywhere, which was unconscious everywhere; and so, the remarkable thing is that things are taking place

AUTOMATICALLY (*gesture of points scattered throughout the world*), quite unexpected things here and there, even in people who don't know anything.

(*silence*)

These material cells had to gain the capacity to receive and manifest the consciousness; and what permits a radical transformation is that instead of an ascent which is so to speak eternal and indefinite, there is the appearance of a new type – a descent from above. The previous descent was a mental one, while this is what Sri Aurobindo calls a "supramental descent"; the impression is, a descent of the supreme Consciousness infusing itself into something capable of receiving and manifesting it. Then, out of that, once it has been thoroughly kneaded (there's no knowing how much time it will take), a new form will be born, which will be the form Sri Aurobindo called supramental – it will be ... anything, I don't know what those beings will be called.

What will be their mode of expression? How will they make themselves understood and so on?... In man, it developed very slowly. Only, mind has done a lot of kneading and, after all, has made things move faster.

How will we get there?... There will certainly be stages in the manifestation with, perhaps, a specimen that will come and say, "Here is how it is." (*Mother looks in front of her*) One can see that.

Only, when man emerged from the animal, there was no way to record – to note and record the process; now it's quite different, so it will be more interesting.

(*silence*)

But even at this moment in time, the vast majority – the vast majority – of human intellectuality is perfectly satisfied being busy with itself, satisfied with its little progress like this (*Mother draws a microscopic circle*). It doesn't even, doesn't even have a desire for something else!

72

Which means the advent of the superhuman being may well ... it may very well go unnoticed, or not be understood. We can't say, because there is no analogy; it's obvious that if one of the apes, the large apes, had met the first man, he would just have felt there was a somewhat ... strange being, that's all. But now it's different because man thinks, reasons....

But anything higher than him man has been used to thinking of as ... divine beings; that is to say, bodiless beings, appearing in the light, anyway all the gods in human conception – but it's not that at all!

(long silence)

...

So?

Aren't you convinced?

Why don't you try?

But I do! That's why I asked you the question. I am not doubting anything. I asked you how it's done, that's what I don't see.... For instance, I shave every morning. Well, in the morning you are dazed, tired, the mind doesn't work, the vital doesn't work....

Yes, it's an excellent opportunity.

Well, yes, so that's what I do! But I tell you, I just don't see, I don't. I don't know how it can be stirred – it doesn't stir.... It doesn't stir unless I apply the mind or the vital or the heart.

Bah!

It's not that I doubt! I say that my body is a donkey, quite possibly, but I don't doubt.

It's not a donkey, poor thing! *(Mother laughs)*

Doubt there isn't. But there is a question on the "how," that's what I don't know.

That problem never arose for me, because ... When you do music or when you do painting, you very clearly notice how the consciousness permeates the cells and those cells become conscious. This experience, for instance: there are objects in a box, and you say to your hand, "Take twelve of them." The hand goes like that, without your bothering about it, and it finds the twelve (without counting, just like that), it takes the twelve and gives them to you. That's an experience I had long ago; when I was twenty I began with experiences of that kind. So I know, I knew how the consciousness works. You understand, it's impossible to learn the piano or painting without the consciousness coming into the hands, and the hands become conscious INDEPENDENTLY of the brain – the brain may be busy elsewhere, it doesn't matter in the least. Besides, that's what happens in those people who are called "sleepwalkers": they have a consciousness belonging to their body, which makes them move about and do things quite independently of the mind and the vital.

I mean that when I am shaving in front of the mirror, if within myself I don't apply the mantra or an aspiration from the heart, well, it's an inert chunk shaving, and in addition the physical mind keeps running. But if I apply a mantra or a mental will ...

No! It's THE BODY that ends up saying the mantra spontaneously! So spontaneously that even if you happen to be thinking of something else, your body will be saying the mantra. Don't you have that experience?

No.

And it's the body that aspires, the body that says the mantra, the body that wants the light, the body that wants the consciousness – you yourself may be thinking of something else, Tom, Dick or Harry or a book or anything, it doesn't matter.

But now I understand, I understand very well! In the beginning I didn't, I thought I had been made supposedly very ill in order to stop the life I led downstairs – the life I now lead is far more busy than the one I led downstairs, so ... I wondered why, whether it was a transitional phase. But now I understand: cut off – I would keep fainting. What made the doctor declare that I was ill is that I couldn't take a step without fainting: if I wanted to walk from here to there, poff! I would faint on the way; I had to be held up so my body wouldn't drop to the ground. So the doctor's decision: to bed and no moving. But as for me, not for one minute did I lose consciousness! I would faint but remain conscious, I would see my body and know I had fainted; I didn't lose consciousness, the body didn't lose consciousness. So now I understand! The body was cut off from the vital and the mind and left to its own means; and then little by little, little by little ...

I remember, for instance, all that the doctors do: they give you vitamins, this and that. All right. So as soon as I had taken those vitamins, I saw that sort of physical mind start stirring and stirring and stirring: "Vitamins," I said, "I don't want them, they cause excitement in the brain." Then they changed and gave me something some other time, and that was good. And all that, all of it was simply THE BODY: all that it knew, all the experiences it had had, all the mastery from all the parts of the being, from the vital to the mind and above, all of that was gone! And this poor body was left to itself. Then, naturally, little by little something was rebuilt. For a long time I remained unable ... unable to do hardly anything (a little something, but hardly anything), but little by little it all was rebuilt, increasingly rebuilt: a conscious, purely conscious being – which is now chattering away! (It was unable to express itself.)

Yes, I understand. I understand. Well, perhaps that is what Sri Aurobindo meant when he said, "Your body is at present the only one on earth that can do this work." I thought it was a kindness on his part.... But it's true that it was cut off, I knew it – I saw it – cut off, the states of being were sent away: "Go away, all of you are not wanted anymore." Then the body had to rebuild a life for itself. And instead of having to go through all those states of being as it did before, through successive awakenings *(gesture of ascent from degree to degree, in the way of the yogis of old)*, up to the highest height, the highest height beyond the form, now it's no longer that at all, the body no longer needs anything of all that, it simply has ... *(gesture of a rising aspiration opening out like a flower)*. Something within opened and developed, which caused that idiotic mind to become organized and capable of falling silent in an aspiration. And then ... then there was the direct Contact, without intermediaries – the direct contact. That it now has constantly. Constantly, every single moment, the direct contact. And it's THE BODY: it doesn't go through all kinds of things and states of being, not at all, it's direct.

But once that has been done (this is something Sri Aurobindo had said), once ONE body has done it, it has the capacity of passing it on to others; and I tell you, there is now (I am not saying in its totality and in detail, probably not), but here and there *(scattered gesture to show various points on earth)* people suddenly get one experience or another. Some of them (most) get frightened, so naturally it goes away – that is because they weren't prepared enough within (if it's not the little routine of every minute, ever the same, they get frightened), and once they get frightened it's over, it means they will need years of preparation for the experience to recur. But still, some don't; suddenly, an experience: "Ah!" something wholly new, wholly unexpected, which they had never thought of.

It's contagious. That I know. And it's the only hope, because if everyone had to go through the same experience again ... Well, I am ninety now – at the age of ninety people are tired, they've had enough of life. To do this work one must feel as young as a small child.

It takes a long time, I clearly see that it has taken a long time.

And it isn't done, of course, it's BEING done – it isn't done, far from it. Far from it ... What's the proportion of conscious cells? We don't know.

From time to time, some cells scold others, that's very funny! They scold them, they catch hold of them, say a thing or two (in their own way) to those which want ... *(Mother draws a tiny circle)* to go on with the old habits: digestion has to be done in a certain way, absorption has to be done in a certain way, circulation has to be done in a certain way, breathing has to ... all the functions have to be done according to Nature's method. And when it isn't like that, they are worried. Then those which know catch hold of them and give them a good bombardment of the Lord, it's very funny!

There is something that translates into words (it's wordless, but something in there translates into words), and so there are conversations between the cells *(Mother laughs)*: "You fool, what are you afraid of? Don't you see it's the Lord doing this to transform you?" Then the other: "Ah! ..." And then it falls quiet, opens out, and waits. And ... the pain goes away, the disorder goes away, and then everything works out.

It's wonderful.

But if by some mischance the mind comes in, starts watching or judging, then everything stops and falls back into the old habit.

(long silence)

Basically, it's the vital, mental – and so on – ego, it's all of that which was – poff! – taken away.

It was a radical operation.

So now there is a sort of suppleness and plasticity. And all this is learning (it's very much in touch with everything *[horizontal gesture]*), it's learning to find its whole support, its whole strength, its whole knowledge, its whole light, its whole will, everything like that *(vertical gesture, turned to the Supreme)*, exclusively like that, in an extraordinary plasticity.

And then – the splendor of the Presence.

(silence)

There.

So what should I do to you?

I don't know, an operation!

A radical operation *(Mother laughs)*.

Yes, perhaps.

But tell me, when they put you to sleep to open your stomach, were you conscious? Nothing at all? Nothing?

No.

We'll see....
We'll see.

The essential character of Supermind is a Truth consciousness which knows by its own inherent right of nature, by its own light: it has not to arrive at knowledge but possesses it. It may indeed, especially in its evolutionary action, keep knowledge behind its apparent consciousness and bring it forward as if from behind the veil; but even then this veil is only an appearance and does not really exist: the knowledge was always there, the consciousness its possessor and present revealer. This too is only in the evolutionary play and on the supramental plane itself the consciousness lives always in an immediacy of knowledge and acts by a direct immediacy of knowledge. In Mind as we see it here the action is very different; it starts from an apparent absence of knowledge, a seeming ignorance or nescience, even, in material Nature, from an inconscience in which any kind of knowing does not seem at all to exist. It reaches knowledge or the action of knowledge by steps which are not at all immediate but rather knowledge at first seems utterly impossible and foreign to the very substance of this Matter. Yet, in the blindness of Matter itself there are signs of a concealed consciousness which in its hidden fundamental being sees and has the power to act according to its vision and even by an infallible immediacy which is inherent in its nature.

This is the same Truth that is apparent in Supermind but is here involved and seems not to be.

JUNE 29, 1968

It's a movement of acceleration: it's the great work of the whole creation to consciously return ("return" is another silly word – "turn to" would be better), to become again, to identify again, not by abolishing the whole work of development and ascent, but ... It's like a multiplication of the facets of Consciousness, and that multiplication is growing increasingly coherent, organized and conscious of itself.

Individualization is only a means to make the innumerable details of the Consciousness more complex, more refined, more coherent. And "individualization" ... we shouldn't mistake it for physical life; physical life is ONE of the various means of that individualization, with such fragmenting and such limitation that it compels a concentration that intensifies the details of the development; but once that is done, it [individualization] isn't the lasting truth.

(*Mother goes into a long contemplation*)

What did you want to tell me?

You say that this individualization isn't the "lasting truth"?

Individualization, in its feeling or perception or impression, in its sense of separate individuality, has no lasting truth. It continues to exist (how should I put it?) in all its power and all its knowledge, but with the sense of Oneness. Which is altogether different. And there is such a clear perception of what comes into the consciousnesses, into the individuals, what comes from the falsehood of separation; there always remains something, but sometimes it grows dim almost to the point of disappearing (that's in exceptional cases or exceptional beings). But the sense of division must completely disappear. It's ...

To explain anything at all I would have to say too many things.

(*contemplation*)

I'll say more another time.

...

But for this body it's interesting: it's in the smallest little details, you know, that the body is shown the extent to which the presence has a real effect, thus making it necessary, and the extent to which it isn't necessary. It's growing increasingly precise in the smallest details.

The cells have no personal choice; their attitude is really like this: "What You will, what You will ..." for everything, everything. With only an increasing, intensifying, more and more constant, uninterrupted sensation that the sole support is – the Supreme Lord. There's only He, only He. And that's inside, in the body.

80

At the same time, a very precise perception.... You know, once (years ago) I was asked, "What is purity?" I answered, "Purity is to be exclusively under the influence of the Supreme Lord and to receive nothing but from him." Then, a year or two later, while reading Sri Aurobindo, I found a sentence in English which said exactly the same thing in other words (a sentence I had never read and didn't know). I saw that same sentence yesterday evening (I have a calendar with quotations from Sri Aurobindo).... They [the cells] are growing purer and purer, and the extent to which they aren't is pointed out very clearly, in an absolutely precise, distinct way, as if with the point of a needle, on the spot that isn't pure. And it hurts! It always corresponds to a pain – while the same physical condition goes on. Take an exposed nerve in a tooth: normally, it should hurt constantly; at times, in an almost general way, it doesn't exist, but just when the purity isn't total, whew! It hurts excruciatingly!... And in a few seconds it may pass. So it all exclusively depends on That – everything. It's a proof, the most concrete proof!

Since, then, eternal and immutable delight of being moving out into infinite and variable delight of becoming is the root of the whole matter, we have to conceive one indivisible conscious Being behind all our experiences supporting them by its inalienable delight and effecting by its movement the variations of pleasure, pain and neutral indifference in our sensational existence.

That is our real self; the mental being subject to the triple vibration can only be a representation of our real self put in front for the purposes of that sensational experience of things which is the first rhythm of our divided consciousness in its response and reaction to the multiple contacts of the universe. It is an imperfect response, a tangled and discordant rhythm preparing and preluding the full and unified play of the conscious Being in us; it is not the true and perfect symphony that may be ours if we can once enter into sympathy with the One in all variations and attune ourselves to the absolute and universal diapason.

JULY 17, 1968

Mother reads a question She has received

"Is the will to progress sufficient to prevent the deterioration that stems from time? How can the physical being prevent this deterioration?"

That's just what the body's transformation is about! It's when the physical cells become not only conscious, but RECEPTIVE to the true Consciousness-Force, that is, when they allow the working of that higher Consciousness. That's the work of transformation.... Not so easy!

JULY 20, 1968

While you were meditating, I've rarely had such a physical impression, such a physical experience, in my body.

Oh?

Yes, I felt it very strongly: something that wasn't at all happening up above, but here.

(Mother nods and remains silent)

Yes, basically like a consciousness here, in the body.

Yes, yes.

(silence)

The extraordinary thing is that with such a ... fantastic torrent of force as the one near you, or on you, or in you, it doesn't find a more physical expression than that!

But more and more (through news people bring or things that happen), I have more and more the sense of such an awesome torrent that ... Yes, I think it's like this: I think everything is changing, and changing with fantastic speed, but we don't notice it and we'll only become aware of it ... afterwards. Because there are hundreds of occasions to note details, and the overall impression is rather stupendous. For instance, if the consciousness is concentrated, if for some reason it's concentrated here in the body, then everything seems as if it's bursting – boiling and bursting – to such a point that I have asked several times, "Do I have a fever?" – I don't have a fever at all! And as soon as there is stillness, inactivity, and a concentration with the consciousness, then it's something so awesome, immense, you know, and ... Then there is Peace, Serenity. A peace ... something inexpressible – in an awesome action. And then ...

(Mother goes into a contemplation)

SEPTEMBER 28, 1968

It's quite certain that when the Supramental manifests, it will replace the ... (what can we call it?) restricting mental precision – a precision which limits, and therefore partly warps things – by a clarity of vision, another kind

83

of precision that will not restrict. That's what is being built.

Ultimately, we might say (this is not exactly the thing) that in order to make things precise, the mind limits and separates them; and there is evidently a precision that can come from a more accurate vision, without division or separation. That precision will be that of the supramental vision. Along with the precision, there will come the vision of the RELATIONSHIP between all things, without separating them.

But that's something being prepared. It comes in a flash, for a minute, then things fall back into their old way.

We could say the same thing for the vital: the vital gives an intensity which nothing else seems capable of giving; well, that same intensity exists in the Supramental, but without division. It's an intensity that doesn't separate things.

I've had both experiences, but in a very short-lived manner. Those are things that are just now being worked out.

The visible imperfections and limitations of mind in the present stage of its evolution here we take as part of its very nature; but in fact the boundaries in which it is still penned are only temporary limits and measures of its still incomplete evolutionary advance; its defects of methods and means are faults of its immaturity and not proper to the constitution of its being; its achievement, although extraordinary under the hampering conditions of the mental being weighed down by its instrumentation in an earthly body, is far below and not beyond what will be possible to it in its illumined future. For mind is not in its very nature an inventor of errors, a father of lies bound down to a capacity of falsehood, wedded to its own mistakes and the leader of a stumbling life as it too largely is at present owing to our human shortcomings: it is in its origin a principle of light, an instrument put forth from the Supermind and, though set to work within limits and even set to create limits, yet the limits are luminous borders for a special working, voluntary and purposive bounds, a surface of the finite ever extending itself under the eye of infinity.

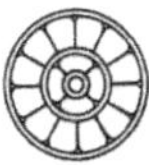

NOVEMBER 27, 1968

I truly don't know if there are "parts" or organs that still have what we might call their "spirit of independence," but truly the body has made its surrender, that is, it has no will of its own; it has no desire, no will of its own, and it's all the time as if "listening" – all the time – to perceive the Indication.

It's beginning to know the exact spot or function that isn't ... I can't say "transformed," because that's quite a high-sounding word, but not in harmony with the others, and causing a disorder. That's becoming a perception of every moment. When something apparently abnormal takes place, there is the understanding, the awareness of why it occurs and what it must be leading to: how an apparent disorder can lead to a greater perfection. That's it. It's a tiny little beginning. But it has begun. The body is beginning to be a little conscious. And not only for itself alone, but for all others too, it has begun: seeing, perceiving how the Consciousness (with a capital

C) acts in others. And in fact, at times (words lag WAY BEHIND the experience), there no longer is the perception of division: there is the perception of diversity (that's becoming very interesting) ... the diversity (if it weren't for what we might call the "latching on" of separateness), the diversity that, in the true consciousness, would be perfectly harmonious and would make a whole that would be perfection itself.

(Mother makes a round gesture).

It's the latching on – what happened?... What happened?...

It remains to be seen if, for some reason or other, it was necessary or if it was an accident – but how could it be an accident! ... For the moment (there's no thought, so it's a little vague), for the moment there is an impression ... I might put it simply like this: the impression of a TREMENDOUS acquisition of consciousness, which has been gained by paying the very high price of all the suffering and all the disorder.... Yesterday or today (I forget when, I think yesterday), at one point the problem was so acute *(Mother touches her cheek and throat),* and then the divine Consciousness seemed to be saying, "In all this suffering, it's I who suffer" (the Consciousness, you understand), "it's I who suffer, but in a way different from yours." I don't know how to express it.... There was a sort of impression that the divine Consciousness was perceiving what to us was a suffering, that it existed – it existed for the divine Consciousness. But not in the same way as it exists for our own consciousness. So then, there was an attempt to make understood the consciousness of the whole at the same time, the simultaneous consciousness of everything ... to express myself I might just say, the consciousness of suffering (the most acute disorder) and of Harmony (the most perfect Ananda) – both together, perceived together. Naturally that changes the nature of suffering.

But all that is very conscious of being some kind of chatter. It's not the translation of what is.

There is also the perception that little by little, following all these experiences, every aggregate (what, for us, is a body) is getting used to having the power to bear the true Consciousness.... It requires a play of adaptation.

But you know, Sri Aurobindo too wrote in Thoughts and Glimpses, I think, that suffering was a preparation for Ananda.

Yes. I must say there are many things from Sri Aurobindo that I am beginning to understand in a very different way.

DECEMBER 21, 1968

Someone (not me) has asked a question. It seems it's "typical" of the questions people ask after reading your "Notes".... Would you like to know?

It must again be something ...

I'll read it to you: "While describing her experiences of last August and September, the Mother refers to the 'exclusion of the mind and vital.' Why do they have to be eliminated for a rapid and effective transformation of the body? Doesn't the supramental consciousness act on them too?"

87

Certainly it acts! It's ALREADY been acting, for a long time. It's because the body is used (was used) to obeying the vital and especially the mind, so it's to change its habit, to make it obey the higher Consciousness alone. That's why. It's to make things go faster. In people, That acts through the mind and vital – and as I said, it's safer that way. As an experience it's rather risky, but it makes things move considerably faster, because normally you must act on the body through those two, whereas in that way, with them absent, That acts directly. That's all.

...

The process isn't to be recommended! Every time I have an opportunity, I say so: people mustn't imagine they should try to do that (they couldn't, but that doesn't matter), it's not recommended. One should take the time needed. But that was because of the number of years ... to make things go faster.

(silence)

The strange thing is that there are kinds of demonstrations of the body's natural tendency (I suppose it's not the same thing for all bodies: it depends on the way it was built, that is, father, mother, antecedents, and so on), a demonstration of the body left to itself. This one, for instance, has a sort of imagination (it's something odd), a dramatic imagination: it constantly feels it's living catastrophes; and then, with its faith, which remains there, the catastrophe is turned into a realization; things of that sort, absurd. So for a while it's left to that imagination (that's what happened these last few days), and when it's sufficiently tired of that idiotic activity, it prays, you know, with all its intensity it prays for it to cease! Instantly, hup! the thing just goes like this *(gesture of reversal)*, it turns around at one stroke, and the body is in a contemplation (not a faraway one, very close) of this wonderful Presence which is everywhere.

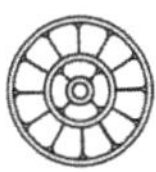

JANUARY 4, 1969

On the 1st, something really strange took place …. And I wasn't the only one to feel it, a few people felt it too. It began just after midnight, but I felt it at 2, and others at 4 in the morning. It was … I told you a few words about it last time, but the surprising thing is that it didn't correspond to anything I expected (I didn't expect anything), or to any of the things I had felt. It was something very material, I mean it was very external – very outward – and luminous, with a golden light. It was very strong, powerful. But its character was a smiling benevolence, a peaceful joy, and a sort of blossoming in the joy and the light. And it was like a "happy new year," like a wish. I must say it took me by surprise.

It lasted – I felt it for at least three hours. Afterwards, I stopped concerning myself with it, I don't know what happened. But I told you a few words about it, and I spoke to two or three others: they had all felt it. Which means it was VERY material. They had all felt a sort of joy like that, but an amiable, powerful joy, and … oh, so sweet, very smiling, VERY BENEVOLENT … something … I don't know what it is. I don't know what it is, but it's a kind of benevolence; so it was something very close to the human. And so concrete! So concrete. As if it had a taste, so concrete was it. Afterwards, I didn't concern myself with it anymore, except that I told two or three people about it: they had all felt it. Now, I don't know whether it has mingled or … It hasn't gone, it doesn't give the feeling of something that comes only to go away.

It was far more external than the things I usually feel, far more external …. Hardly mental at all, I mean there was

no sense of a "promise" or … No. It would rather be like …
My own impression was that of an immense personality,
immense (meaning that for it, the earth was small, like this
[Mother holds a small object in the hollow of her hands],
like a ball), an immense personality, so very benevolent,
and coming to … (Mother seems to gently raise the little
ball in the hollow of her hands). It was the impression of
a personal god (yet it was … I don't know) who comes to
help. So very strong! And so sweet at the same time, so
understanding.

And it was very external: the body felt it everywhere,
everywhere (Mother touches her face, her hands), all over
like this.

What has become of it? I don't know.

It was the start of the year. As if someone on the scale
of a god (someone, that is) had come to say "Happy new
year," with all the power to make it a happy year. It was
like that.

But what was it? …

So concrete …

I don't know.

Is it … is it the personality (because it didn't have any
form, I didn't see any form, there was only what it brought
along [Mother feels the atmosphere with her fingers],
sensation and feeling, these two things – sensation
and feeling), I wondered if it wasn't the supramental
personality … which will, then, manifest later in material
forms?

Since then, the body – this body – has been feeling
(it has been permeated by that everywhere, a lot), it has
been feeling much more joyful and less concentrated,
living more in a happy, smiling expansion. For instance,
it speaks more easily. There's a note … a constant note of
benevolence. A smile, you know, a benevolent smile, and
all that with a GREAT FORCE …. I don't know.

Haven't you felt anything?

That day, I had a sense of contentment.

Ah, that's it! Yes, that's right.

Is it the supramental personality? ... Which will incarnate in all those who will have a supramental body ...?

It was luminous, smiling, and so benevolent because of its POWER: I mean that generally, benevolence in the human being is something slightly weak, in the sense that it doesn't like battle, it doesn't like struggle – but this wasn't like that at all! A benevolence that imposes itself (Mother brings her two fists down on the armrests of her chair).

It interested me because it was entirely new. And so concrete! Concrete like this (Mother touches the arms of her chair), like what the physical consciousness usually regards as "others," as concrete as that. Which means it didn't come through some inner being, through the psychic being: it came DIRECTLY onto the body.

What is it? ... Yes, it may be that .... The body's feeling since that took place has been a sort of certitude; a certitude as if now it no longer were in an anxiety or uncertainty to know. "What will it be? What will this Supramental PHYSICALLY be like?" the body used to wonder. "What will it be like physically?" Now, it no longer thinks about it, it's happy.

Very well.

Is it something that's going to permeate the bodies that are ready?

Yes ... I think so, yes. I feel it's the formation that's going to permeate and express itself – permeate and express itself – in the bodies ... which will be the bodies of the Supramental.

Or maybe … maybe the superman? I don't know. The intermediary between the two. Maybe the superman: it was very human, but a human of divine proportions, you understand.

A human without weaknesses and shadows: it was all luminous – all light and smile and … sweetness at the same time.

Yes, maybe the superman.

(silence)

I don't know why, for a moment I have been thinking insistently: people who won't know how things actually happened will say, once this supramental force has entered the earth's atmosphere and penetrated them, they will say, "Well, WE are the ones who did this!"

(Mother laughs) Yes, probably!

It's we, it's our fine humanity that has … blossomed.

Yes, certainly It's always like that.

That's why I say – I say that after all, for all of us here who have to face all the difficulties, it's really a Grace! Because WE will know how – and we will not cease to be, of course.

We will know how it was done.

The silent Soul of all the world was there:
A Being lived, a Presence and a Power,
A single Person who was himself and all
And cherished Nature's sweet and dangerous throbs
Transfigured into beats divine and pure.
One who could love without return for love,
Meeting and turning to the best the worst,
It healed the bitter cruelties of earth,
Transforming all experience to delight;
Intervening in the sorrowful paths of birth
It rocked the cradle of the cosmic Child
And stilled all weeping with its hand of joy;
It led things evil towards their secret good,
It turned racked falsehood into happy truth;
Its power was to reveal divinity.
Infinite, coeval with the mind of God,
It bore within itself a seed, a flame,
A seed from which the Eternal is new-born,
A flame that cancels death in mortal things.
All grew to all kindred and self and near;
The intimacy of God was everywhere,
No veil was felt, no brute barrier inert,
Distance could not divide, Time could not change.
A fire of passion burned in spirit-depths,
A constant touch of sweetness linked all hearts,
The throb of one adoration's single bliss
In a rapt ether of undying love.
An inner happiness abode in all,
A sense of universal harmonies,
A measureless secure eternity
Of truth and beauty and good and joy made one.
Here was the welling core of finite life;
A formless spirit became the soul of form.

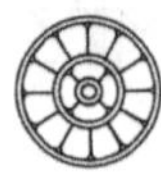

And this descent of the superman consciousness …
Did I tell you I had afterwards identified it?

When you spoke last time, you had identified it.

Yes, but I spoke of "supramental consciousness."

Later, you said, "Maybe the superman?"

Yes, that's it. It's the descent of the superman consciousness. I had the assurance of it afterwards.

It was on the Ist of January after midnight. I woke up at 2 in the morning, surrounded by a consciousness, but so concrete, and NEW, in the sense that I had never experienced that. It lasted, quite concrete and present, for two or three hours, and then it spread out and went to find all those who could receive it. And at the same time I knew it was the consciousness of the superman, that is, the intermediary between man and the supramental being.

It has given the body a sort of assurance, a sort of trust. That experience has made it steady, as it were, and if it keeps the true attitude, all the support is there to help it.

A certain number of people (I asked afterwards) had the experience, they felt it (not as clearly), felt the presence of a new consciousness – lots of people. They told me (I asked them if they had felt something), they told me, "Oh, yes!" But each with … (Mother twists her fingers slightly) naturally his own special approach.

(silence)

The curious thing (I've noticed it with others) is that when the Action is silent, it's FAR MORE PRECISE than when it takes place through words. Words are received mentally, and there is always a slight distortion: a distortion of the content of those words. Whereas when the action is direct (Mother makes a gesture of inner communication), it's very precise.

I don't want to give names, but I've had both examples these last few days. There was someone I was to see only a few days later, so then I put the Consciousness and Force on him, and the change took place, but very clearly and precisely; while to others I spoke of this experience, and they transcribed it: two transcriptions were read out to me, very different from each other (while I very nearly said the same thing), each transcription is different, and there is a slight distortion, different too, in each.

I didn't correct them because words themselves distort, so …

You see, when I speak, I give words a very precise meaning – very subtle and precise; the other person receives the sound of the word and gives it his own interpretation. But what can we do?

This Consciousness takes on a different "color," so to speak, in everyone. It's the same thing with words: words have a similar, but nevertheless different meaning for each of those who utter them …. We would have to communicate like this (gesture of inner exchange): the direct experience.

JANUARY 15, 1969

It has remained, this [superman] consciousness. It has remained, it's very strong, oh! … Today again, with these [Jain] sadhus, I had the experience: it came, mon petit, it was tremendous! It came massively, it enveloped me completely, so I sat very still, like that, behind it: nothing could get through. Interesting … Oh, it really is a power. Down to the vital. Physically, the body cannot respond; there is indeed an action, but … it's not that. It's not that. But it has put a vital in the body (you know that the vital had gone away), an awesome vital! That's quite amusing. You feel as if you were saying to people, "Keep still!"

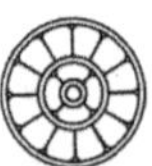

JANUARY 18, 1969

(Regarding the "descent of the superman consciousness.)

Oh, did I tell you? The other day, when the [Jain] sadhu came, as soon as he came in (he stood there), this atmosphere came from here up to there *(Mother draws a half circle in front of her)*, it surrounded me like a wall. It was thick, luminous, and what strength it had! But then, it was wholly directed at him *(gesture of forward projection)*. For me, it was visible, very material, like a rampart, about this thick *(gesture: about a foot and a half)*, and it remained there as long as he was there. It was as if to keep him still! *(Mother laughs)* It was very amusing.

So this consciousness is very consciously active.

(silence Mother gives flowers)

Here, this is for you.

You see (Mother shows two hibiscus flowers), it's not the same thing: this is "Grace," and this is "Supramental Consciousness" – we have the flower before the consciousness!

(silence)

Today I saw Pondicherry's lieutenant governor (he comes now and then, every two weeks), and other people (a guard of Auroville, who is a Muslim), a bit of everything, and now this consciousness comes: the other day, I told you, it was like a rampart, but today with the governor it was much smaller, of limited proportions (*gesture like a beam*), but it was there, intact: it was the same thing, only the concentration was less. And it comes between the Action (*Mother points to her own body*) and the person. It's like a projection of power. And now it has become habitual.

There is in it a consciousness (something VERY precious) that gives lessons to the body, teaches it what it has to do, that is, the attitude it should have, the reaction it should have …. I had already told you a few times how difficult it is to find the procedure of the transformation when there's no one to give you indications; and it's the response, as it were: "he" comes and tells the body, "Have this attitude, do this, do that in that way." So then the body is happy, it's quite reassured, it can't make a mistake anymore.

Very interesting.

It has come like a "mentor" – and PRACTICAL, wholly practical: "This is to be rejected; this is to be accepted; this is to be generalized; this for all inner movements. And it even becomes very material, in the sense that with certain vibrations, it says, "This is to be encouraged"; with others, "This is to be channeled"; with yet others, "This is to be got rid of …." Small indications of that sort.

(silence)

Years ago, in one of the old Talks, when I spoke there, at the Playground, I said, "The superman will probably be first a being of power, so as to be able to defend himself." That's it, it's that experience. It has come back as an experience. And it's because it has come back as an experience that I remembered having said it.

Yes, you said, "Power's what will come first."

Yes, Power first.

Because those beings will need to be protected.

Yes, that's right. Well, I've had the first experience for this body: it came like a rampart, it was awesome! An awesome power! Quite out of proportion with the apparent action.
Very interesting.
And that's also why (now that I see this experience), I see that the result is far more precise and concrete, because the mind and the vital aren't there. Because it [this new consciousness] is taking their place. And with this whole tranquil assurance of knowledge that comes at the same time. It's interesting.

(silence)

Do you have something to say?

I was wondering how, individually, this consciousness will act, for instance outside you?

In the same way. Only, those who haven't made it a habit to observe themselves objectively will notice it less, that's all. It will go through cotton wool, as it were, as it always does. But otherwise it's in the same way.

I mean, this consciousness will not act on the mind so much as on bodies?

I do hope it will make people THINK correctly …

It's a guide, basically.

A guide, yes.
It's a consciousness, you understand.
For me, THE Consciousness limits itself to special activities, in special cases, but it's always THE Consciousness; just as it's almost completely limited in the human consciousness, so too in certain states of being, certain activities, it limits itself to a certain way of being so as to accomplish His action. And that's something I had asked for a lot: "May I be guided every minute," because it saves a huge amount of time, of course, instead of having to study, to observe, to … one knows. Well, now I realize it has happened like that.

(silence)

There is a very pronounced change in those who were touched on the 1st of January: there is especially … as I said, a precision and a certainty that have entered their way of thinking.

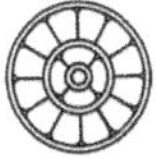

JANUARY 22, 1969

Oh, but this consciousness is very interesting! It gives me lessons all the time, it's very interesting!
He gives me lessons during the night to tell me the things that must change, and with symbolic sounds to

make me clearly understand: he makes me LIVE certain situations to know what needs to be changed – what he does is first-rate!

It's going on in every detail. I can't tell everything.

And it doesn't just concern itself with individuals: it also concerns itself with events all over the world. I see that clearly because it intervenes in the action of this or that nation, I see that mostly at night.

It's very active.

He's educating me! Educating this body. That's really very fine!

(Mother laughs) We'll see what's going to happen it depends on the body's plasticity, of course.

FEBRUARY 15, 1969

Just one thing, this atmosphere, this [superman] Consciousness is very active, and active like a mentor, as I already told you. And it's going on. One of these last few mornings, for a few hours early in the morning, it was … Never, never had the body been so happy! It was the complete Presence, absolute freedom, and a certitude: these cells, other cells *(gesture here and there showing other bodies)*, it didn't matter, it was life everywhere, consciousness everywhere.

Absolutely wonderful.

It came effortlessly, and it left simply because … I was too busy. It doesn't come at will – what comes at will is what we might call a "copy": it looks like it, but it's not

THE Thing. The Thing ... There is something wholly independent of our aspiration, our will, our effort ... wholly independent. And this something appears to be absolutely all-powerful, in the sense that none of the body's difficulties exists. At such times, everything disappears. Aspiration, concentration, effort ... no use at all. And it's the DIVINE SENSE, you understand, that's what having the divine sense means. During these few hours (three or four hours), I understood in an absolute way what having the divine consciousness in the body means. And then, this body, that body, that other body ... *(gesture here and there, all around Mother)*, it doesn't matter: it moved about from one body to another, quite free and independent, aware of the limitations or the possibilities of each body-absolutely wonderful, I had never, ever had this experience before. Absolutely wonderful. It left because I was so busy that ... and it didn't leave because it had just come to show "how it is" – that's not it: it's because life and the organization of life *(gesture like a truckload being dumped)* engulf you.

I know it's there *(gesture in the background)*, I know it is, but ... But that's a transformation as I understand it! And clearly, in people it could express itself-not something vague, clearly – in this man, in that woman, in ... (same gesture here and there), quite clearly. And with a Smile!
...

The cells themselves were saying their effort to be transformed, and there was a Calm .... (How can I explain this? ...) The body was saying its aspiration and will to prepare itself, and, not asking but striving to be what it should be; all that always with this question (it's not the body that asks it, it's ... the environment, those around -the world, as if the world were asking the question): "Will it continue, or will it have to dissolve? ..." The body is like this *(gesture of abandon, hands open upward)*, it says, "What You will, Lord." But then, it knows the question is decided, and One doesn't want to tell it – it accepts. It doesn't lose patience, it accepts, it says, "Very well, it will be as You will." But That which knows and That which doesn't answer is ... something that can't be expressed. It is ... yes, I think the only word that can describe the sensation it gives is "an Absolute" – an Absolute. Absolute. That's the sensation: of being in the presence of the Absolute. The Absolute: absolute Knowledge, absolute Will, absolute Power ... Nothing, nothing can resist. And then this Absolute (there's this sensation, concrete) is so merciful! But if we compare it with all that we regard as goodness, mercy ... ugh! that's nothing at all. It's THE Mercy with the absolute power and ... it's not Wisdom, not Knowledge, it's ... It has nothing to do with our process. And That is everywhere, it's everywhere. It's the body's experience. And to That it has given itself entirely, totally, without asking anything – anything. A single aspiration *(same gesture, hands open upward)*, "To be capable of being That, what That wills, of serving That" – not even "serving," of BEING That.

But that state, which lasted for several hours ... never had this body, in the ninety-one years it's been on earth, felt such happiness: freedom, absolute power, and no limits *(gesture here and there and everywhere)*, no limits, no impossibilities, nothing. It was ... all other bodies were itself. There was no difference, it was only a play of the consciousness ... *(gesture like a great Rhythm)* moving about.

So there.

Apart from that, all the rest is as usual.

Appearance looked back to its hidden truth
And made of difference oneness' smiling play;
It made all persons fractions of the Unique,
Yet all were being's secret integers.
All struggle was turned to a sweet strife of love
In the harmonised circle of a sure embrace.
Identity's reconciling happiness gave
A rich security to difference.
On a meeting line of hazardous extremes
The game of games was played to its breaking-point,
Where through self-finding by divine self-loss
There leaps out unity's supreme delight
Whose blissful undivided sweetness feels
A communality of the Absolute.
There was no sob of suffering anywhere;
Experience ran from point to point of joy:
Bliss was the pure undying truth of things.
All Nature was a conscious front of God:
A wisdom worked in all, self-moved, self-sure,
A plenitude of illimitable Light,
An authenticity of intuitive Truth,
A glory and passion of creative Force.
Infallible, leaping from eternity,
The moment's thought inspired the passing act.
A word, a laughter, sprang from Silence' breast,
A rhythm of Beauty in the calm of Space,
A knowledge in the fathomless heart of Time.

NOVEMBER 15, 1969

Have you brought anything special? … Me, I have nothing, except a very small thing, which is that last night, for the first time, for about two hours continuously (I was simply as I always am, like that, quiet), the Force … I seemed to be like a sponge. I don't know how to explain: it's not that it was coming "from above," or like this (horizontal gesture), but it was coming in – I was like a pipe – and then going out ceaselessly, ceaselessly … For one hour, the Force, with an intense golden color, went out like that, and then spread over the world. It's the first time I have felt it physically – I felt physically. And it had such extraordinary power! And this [the body], it was as if I were … a water tap or a pipe, you understand, but it didn't come from a precise spot: it was as though I were immersed in it, and, through me, it flowed and flowed (gesture through Mother and spreading out everywhere). It went on for more than two hours early this morning, that is, between one and four (I don't know exactly); my impression is that it lasted for more than two and a half hours like that. And I saw the Force. The body only acted as a way to touch the earth – the Force came, then it went out and spread. And it went … I saw that, I saw it go towards all those who call. It was directed by a wholly conscious consciousness, while I was … quiet, (laughing) I just was the pipe!

It's the only thing I had to say.

It's the first time it has happened physically, it was physical.

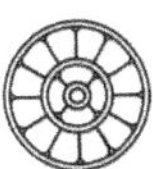

NOVEMBER 19, 1969

…I could note that all the work *(Mother's daily customary work)* could be done without the consciousness being altered. That's not what altered my consciousness: what veiled my consciousness was seeing people; that was when I began being here and doing what I do every day: projecting the divine Consciousness on people.

But it has come back … (what could I call it?) on the fringe, I mean that instead of BEING in it, when you asked me I began perceiving it. But the sensation is no longer there – there was nothing left BUT THAT, you understand! There was nothing left but that, and everything, everything had changed – in appearance, in meaning, in …

That must be the supramental consciousness, I think that's what the supramental consciousness is.

The Immobile stands behind each daily act,
A background of the movement and the scene,
Upholding creation on its might and calm
And change on the Immutable's deathless poise.
The Timeless looks out from the travelling hours;
The Ineffable puts on a robe of speech
Where all its words are woven like magic threads
Moving with beauty, inspiring with their gleam,
And every thought takes up its destined place
Recorded in the memory of the world.
The Truth supreme, vast and impersonal
Fits faultlessly the hour and circumstance,

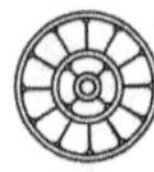

DECEMBER 3, 1969

What I said about the supramental consciousness, is it clear?

I think it's very clear!

Because when I spoke to you, I wasn't in it, it was only a memory.

But it's clear, I could read it to you.

We'll see.

How to express that? … What I lived was that there was NOTHING but this Consciousness; now … it's not a memory, it has stayed on – it has stayed on, but it's veiled, so it expresses itself THROUGH the usual consciousness which is there *(gesture above the head)*. The usual consciousness is there. And this Consciousness really has an interesting effect on the body, because in this body, with the elements that were there, it has built a vital and a mind. Now I've found that the body feels as it used to feel before, that is to say in full possession of its faculty But the mind and vital are no longer independent in the sense that they do as they like – they are under the complete control of the Consciousness. Then the body still has spots of timidity, but it's beginning to recapture the state it was in before …. It's a very slow and long work, but … I don't know how long it will take, but once it reaches a certain perfection, the body will once again be capable of many things it had lost because of that [the departure of the mind and vital]. It wasn't a physical deterioration, that's what deprived it, and it's beginning to slowly, slowly come back.

We'll see.

But it's a long and slow work.

(silence)

Formerly, they were the body's masters, so that's what was needed: they had to go away It was through them that the psychic and all the rest used to work – now, that's over: it's direct. But then, the body's possibilities are multiplying again – intensifying, multiplying.

Now, I am all the time (I don't know, at least ten times a day) asked questions, and the answer comes instantly, like this *(gesture of descent)*, with an ease I never had before. All it takes is a few seconds of attention, and it comes. And the answers are much bolder – something that touches an inner truth and isn't bothered by external reactions. The words are much bolder than before, much clearer … Sometimes, when I write them, I say to myself that it would be amusing if you could see them – most of the time it's quite personal things, but the form is interesting.

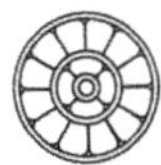

MARCH 28, 1970

This morning for two or three hours, I had a curious experience (the body). Once it had the experience that each … (what could I call it? It wasn't a person, it was like an individualized aggregate), each aggregate had its own essential way (not as it is now, as it IS or ought to be), its own way of understanding and manifesting the Supreme, the Divine, and that was what made its own individuality, its particular way of being. And all those ways put together were roughly a reproduction of the total Divine – but each way has to understand that it's only ONE way and that all other ways are just as true as itself. But it was the body which understood that! It felt it very clearly, for several hours. ONE way … And then, it was so amusing, because *(laughing)* it said, "Yes, yes, as for me, I am the way that wants EVERYTHING to be harmonious!" It said that, repeated it again and again: "I am the way that wants EVERYTHING to be harmonious...." It understood, it understood that; it didn't bother it in the least that there should be millions and billions of other ways – that was ITS way.

Everything, but everything should be harmonious – harmony, harmony, harmony. Something … (words are very, very dry, very hollow) something – a vibration it knows well, a vibration which, for it, is … the expressed combination of Love and Harmony. But "love" is small and "harmony" is small. The two together (along with something else) make up its way of being in the universe.

That was very amusing. Really very amusing.

It understands very, very well – very well – that all have the same right to existence and must … Everything is hardly capable of expressing That which must be expressed.

It was the body, not the mind – strangely, it has a sense of reality that isn't mental or vital or emotive or anything of the sort. It's something else. Very, very concrete.

It's odd.

The body was happy, very happy! It says, "Yes, this is it, this is it!" As if the Lord had told it its secret. It said, "Now I know, now I know this is it." And everyone – everyone and everything – everyone, each of these billions … all of it. But they don't know! *(Mother laughs)*

The body is amusing, you know! As an experience, it was amusing.

Harmony, love. But... what people put into these words isn't the thing – it's not the thing.

(silence)

It's after reading all these Aphorisms: that makes it work a lot.

What should be my way of being?

Ah, it's for you to find it! Oh, that's the only way it's amusing. I think I know, but there it's no longer the body that knows *(Mother makes a gesture above)*. No.... You have to find it. *(Mother laughs)*

108

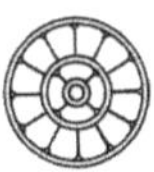

JULY 17, 1970

But what's growing very clear is that all things remaining the same, the position of the consciousness remaining the same, there's a reversal this way or that way *(Mother tips her hand over to one side or another)*, I don't know how to explain. In one case, that is, to the ordinary human consciousness (not ordinary but present), the suffering is almost intolerable; and everything remaining IDENTICALLY the same, with this slight reversal (I don't know how to explain it … maybe we could say "the contact with the Divine," I don't know), but everything remaining the same (it's a phenomenon of consciousness), a wonderful bliss – you understand, physical things remain IDENTICAL!… I have that all the time. Unfortunately … *(laughing)* the painful side lasts longer! When I am in peace, still, then naturally it's the other side.

But this toothache and all that, which to the material consciousness, from an external standpoint, is very real (!), even that is no longer … When the consciousness becomes true, it no longer has the same character – I don't know how to explain. There must be what in our ordinary consciousness we would call a "cure," but it's not a cure: the nature of it changes.

That's the most constant work, that's the work I am in (that's why I have nothing to say).... There are no more ideas, no more feelings, almost no more sensations, it's … this and that *(same gesture of tipping over to one side or to the other)*, this kind of shift, and a shift SO VERY different, you know, and in total immobility!

But in this true consciousness, matter … seems to lose something, or else something is transmuted into … I don't know.... Will it be so permanently, or is it the transition? I don't know. I mean, will the supramental body have no … Yet, there's no difference between man's materiality and the animal's, or is there?

No, Mother, there isn't.

(silence)

When you look, you always reach the same conclusion: you know nothing.

But there is this Consciousness ... all of a sudden, when you no longer ARE, when there's nothing but That, this Consciousness there *(gesture around the head)*, a slightly golden Consciousness, you REALLY get the impression of omnipotence and ... And here you know NOTHING! Nothing, nothing at all, you can't explain anything. All that is ... what I call mental imaginings.

Now, when I am asked a question, nothing, nothing responds, and then all of a sudden the answer comes *(gesture of descent)* in words; but if I am not very attentive, prrt! nothing remains, I can't even recapture the words.... The consciousness of the answer is there *(gesture above)*, it doesn't budge, it's always there, this consciousness, but the materialization of it is very fleeting.

JULY 25, 1970

I must say that two days ago, I had an experience (it was with R. again, she was here), an experience of the whole universe, like a general vision of an Immensity, and then, suddenly the consciousness seemed to become a point taking up no room, and that point was the Eternal Consciousness. But then, it was so strong! So strong ... how all this, this whole unfolded universe was the result of this Consciousness *(Mother shows a point)*. You understand, the consciousness here became this Eternal Consciousness (for a few seconds perhaps, I don't think it lasted even a minute, but time had nothing to do with it), it was the

Eternal, it was the Consciousness. And that experience already prepared something [in Mother], because the two were simultaneous; one didn't abolish the other, the two were simultaneous: this Point that was taking up no room but was eternal, was everything, and at the same time, the unfolding [of the universe]. That was a very intense experience. Then there only remained this vagueness that is the "whole," but it didn't lose its impression of vagueness, that is to say, of something imprecise. Since that time, there has been something changed [in Mother]. And today, in this consciousness, when the answer came, it wasn't the knowledge of "that" – it wasn't the knowledge, it was the working. All of a sudden, I had BECOME the working. So then, I expressed it as best I could in this notebook.... It had such simplicity, you know, a marvelous, all-powerful simplicity!

Words are approximations. I had to use words because I had to write for him, but the experience came like that, the working: the experience of this universal Immensity returning to the Divine Consciousness, how it returns – and innumerably, of course, with all possible experiences, but with a marvelous sim-plic-i-ty.

(long silence)

Words …

It gave me at the same time a sort of bodily experience of the universal movement of the return of the consciousness towards the Divine; and that … a perception that wasn't mental at all, not at all, as if all the cells felt this movement, you understand, this movement of immense return towards the Consciousness.

It must be the movement of the universe towards the Supreme.

I must say that certain things contributed to the experience: in answer to certain questions, yesterday Z told me about the age of the earth, and how they have now managed to measure it (things that are the mental approach to the problem), and suddenly, when he spoke, suddenly there came this sort of union and … (what should I say?) almost a sensation, in the body, of the earth returning to the Divine Consciousness. So the conjunction, combination of all that resulted in this experience.

(silence)

Previously when I used to have experiences (long ago, years ago), it was the mind that benefited more or less, and then it would spread it, use it; now it's not like that: it's directly the body, it's the body that has the experience, and it's MUCH TRUER. There's an intellectual attitude that puts a kind of veil or … I don't know, something … something unreal on the perception of things – an attitude, it's an attitude. It's like seeing through a certain veil or a certain … something … a certain atmosphere, whereas the body feels the thing in itself, it BECOMES that. It feels in itself. It's not as if the thing were taken like this *(gesture of absorption in oneself)*, it's as if the body itself BECAME that *(gesture of bursting or expansion)*. Instead of shrinking the experience down to the individuals scale, the individual widens to the scale of the experience.

(Mother goes into a contemplation) Do you have anything to say?

Once I had a sort of perception which really was an experience, very strong, of this whole universal movement of return, and I had the impression or sensation that everything goes TOWARDS That, everything is FOR That, that it's impossible for anything in all this to be "against," for anything not to go in THAT direction, even when apparently it is "against" or "twisted" or "dark" or …

Yes, yes.

I had the impression that everything goes, is FOR That, there's nothing against – the impossibility of anything against in all this.

112

Yes, it's as if … I don't know … as if the "against" made it nonexistent, you know, in a way incomprehensible to us. An incomprehension that makes us say "against."

It came to me in this form: even what we call the "wrong path" is part of the right path.

Yes.

It looks like a paradox....

Yes, exactly, its a limitation of vision, quite simply.

(silence)

With the perception of space (which must correspond to something), things move away (in what I saw, my experience), they move away as if to follow a vaster curve in order to … That's it: the move away is to broaden one's horizon or field of action.

(silence)

But the interesting thing (very interesting for me) is that the body was very preoccupied with all the difficulties of the transformation, and this experience has given it … I can't call it a "joy" (it's something infinitely superior and greater, stronger – it's so immense!...), as if all the cells were dancing with joy. That's the impression.

These last few days too, I wondered why the body is so absorbed in the difficulties of the transformation, and I received no answer, except to be patient and tranquil and not to fret – as always. But now I understand!... It can only be joyful in a certain atmosphere of truth; then … everything seems to broaden, to relax, and then there's an extraordinary joy with no equivalent in the ordinary perception, none at all.

(Laughing) It's a bit as if someone had taken my head and turned it around! *(Mother turns her head upward)*. You know, this *(gesture above)* is where the Consciousness is, so the head was taken and turned the right way! *(laughter)*

(silence)

It's limitations that create the sense of evil, of bad – as soon as you do away with the limitations, it's gone.

JULY 1, 1970

I had an experience which I found interesting, because it was the first time. It was yesterday or the day before (I forget), R. [Rijuta, an American disciple] was here, just in front of me, kneeling, and I saw her psychic being towering above by this much *(gesture about eight inches)*, taller. It's the first time. Her physical being was short, and the psychic being was tall, like this. And it was a sexless being: neither man nor woman. So I said to myself (it may be always that way, I don't know, but at that time I noticed it very clearly), I said to myself, "But the psychic being is the one that will materialize and become the supramental being!"

I saw it, it was like that. There were distinctive features, but not very pronounced, and it was clearly a being that was neither male nor female, that had features of both combined. And it was taller than her, it exceeded her on every side by about this much *(gesture extending beyond the physical being by about eight inches)*. She was here, and it was like this *(gesture)*. Its color was … this color that, if it became very material, would be Auroville's color [orange]. It was softer, as if behind a veil, it wasn't absolutely precise, but it was this color. And there was hair, but … it was something else.

Another time maybe I'll see better.

But I found it very interesting, because that being seemed to tell me, "You're wondering what the supramental being

114

will be – here it is! Here it is, this is it." And it was there. It was her psychic being.

Then one understands. One understands: the psychic being will materialize ... and it gives a continuity to evolution.

This creation gives you a clear impression that nothing is arbitrary, that there is a sort of divine logic behind, which isn't like our human logic, but highly superior to our logic (but it exists), and that logic was fully satisfied when I saw that.

It's odd, it was also when [Rijuta] was here that I had that experience of the supramental light going through within [Mother] without causing any shadow. [Rijuta] has something like that, I don't know.... And this time, it's really interesting. I was quite interested. It was there, tranquil, and saying to me, "But you're after ... well, here it is, this is it!"

So then, I understood why the mind and the vital were sent away from this body, and the psychic being was left (naturally, it was the psychic being that governed all movements earlier, so it was nothing new, but there were no more difficulties: all the complications coming from the vital and the mind, which add their imprints, their tendencies, it was all gone). So I understood: "Ah, that's it, it's this psychic being that is to become the supramental being."

I had never bothered to know what it looked like. But when I saw that, I understood. And I see it, I still see it, I have kept the memory. Its hair almost looked red, strangely (it wasn't like red hair, but it looked like it). And its expression! Such a fine expression, gently ironical ... oh, extraordinary, extraordinary!

You understand, my eyes were open, it was an almost material vision.

Then one understands! All at once, all questions vanished, it became very clear, very simple.

(silence)

And the psychic is precisely what lives on. So if it materialized, it means doing away with death. But "doing away" ... what's done away with is only what's not according to the Truth, that's what goes away – all that's incapable of being transformed in the image of the psychic, of being part of the psychic.

That's really interesting.

NOVEMBER 17, 1971

(In the radical change of vision you speak of, what makes the difference?

(after a long, smiling silence)

It's as if the consciousness were not in the same position with respect to things – I don't know how to say it. So they seem completely different.

(silence)

I don't know how to explain it.... The ordinary human consciousness, even in people who are broad-minded and all that, is always at the center, and things are like this *(gesture converging from all sides toward a center)*, you understand. Things exist (words reduce everything), things exist in relation to a center. While here ... *(Mother drops a multitude of points throughout space).*

Yes, that's what expresses it the best, I think: in the ordinary human consciousness, you're at one point and everything exists in its relation to that point of

116

consciousness *(same star-shaped gesture)*. While now, the point no longer exists, so things are selfexistent. The point is no longer the source. That's the closest (that's not it, but ...). You see, my consciousness is IN things – it isn't "something that receives" (it's much better than that, but I don't know how to put it into words).

It's better than that because it isn't just "in things": it's in "something" which is in things and which ... moves them.

I could be flowery; I could say (but that's not it): it's no longer one being among other beings, it's ... it's the Divine in everything. But that's not the way I feel it. It's what moves things or what is conscious in things. "What is conscious".... It isn't exactly "governs" because the word "govern" doesn't convey the right sense – "animates" (not that either, all those words reduce and materialize the experience).

(silence)

Evidently, it's a matter of consciousness, but not consciousness as human beings ordinarily have: it's the QUALITY of the consciousness that has changed.

There's a phenomenon, for example (among many others), a curious phenomenon: when I am like that, the consciousness in things, in movements, in life, and I eat lunch, the food is ... there's no effort ... *(Mother remains silent)*. It's too difficult to say.... I don't feel "I" am eating, you see, so I am not aware of putting things in my mouth and having to swallow them and....

Yes, I understand.

I can't say, but the fact is like this: in the new consciousness, I eat very easily, without noticing it, and everything goes very well; as soon as I become conscious in the old consciousness, which means eating, tasting the food, putting it in my mouth – it's difficult! I have all the trouble in the world not to swallow wrong.

It's really something new because I don't know how to describe it.

But then it's extremely concrete: when I am in that consciousness, my whole lunch is taken effortlessly, without any difficulty; I am given food, I swallow and I don't notice ... not that I don't notice it (I have taste, I have everything), but the position is different.

Yes, at that moment it's part of the universal movement.

No, it's something which is at once in me and IN THE FOOD, which tastes and takes, but is no longer ... it's no longer the way it was before, that's all I can say.

It's really new.

And it's particularly noticeable for food, because when I am in that consciousness – which comes as soon as I don't do anything, as soon as I sit quietly – it isn't like something that "comes in" *(gesture toward a center)*, it's like something *(expanding gesture)* ... which develops, which is free to develop. Well then – then it's very good. But if I am in the ordinary consciousness and I eat (it's "time" for a meal), oh, it's so difficult that I feel it's going to be impossible to eat anything! And in the other case, it goes down without my even noticing it. And yet I am conscious of what I am eating.

But what I am saying now isn't it. It's something else.... You see, the consciousness is still like this *(gesture of oscillating from one side to the other)*. Both are there. So.... But then I can't find a way to make myself understood, because new words would have to be invented.

That's increasing from day to day.

It's like at night: I don't sleep and I am not awake; I go into a state in which I don't sleep at all – yet I am not awake. And I don't know how to describe what it is. And when it's normal, it could ... it can last indefinitely, there's no sense of time or fatigue or duration. When the old consciousness comes back, there's almost unbearable suffering: I am suffocating or I can't breathe, or it's a consciousness which shouldn't be there anymore. So quite naturally and effortlessly, I am in the new state, but if I am drawn into the old consciousness by circumstances, it becomes almost unbearable. You see. And it results in pains in the body or ... a body malfunction. But when I enter the new consciousness, everything takes place quite ... without my even noticing it and without any effort.

That's all I can say for the moment.

You see, my body is full of pains and malfunctions, but as soon as I go into that state *(vast, peaceful gesture)* everything is done – time doesn't exist anymore. Time is endless in the old consciousness, while it doesn't exist in this one. I don't know how to describe it.

(silence)

Being flowery, I would say: the old consciousness is like ... it's death, it's as if you were going to die any minute: you suffer, you ... it's the consciousness that leads to death. And the other one (vast, immutable, smiling gesture) is life ... peaceful life, eternal life. Yes, that's it.

But it's not that, you follow, these are just words.

(Mother goes into contemplation)

I can't express it.

THE INDWELLING UNIVERSAL

I contain the wide world in my soul's embrace:
   In me Arcturus and Belphegor burn.
   To whatsoever living form I turn
I see my own body with another face.

All eyes that look on me are my sole eyes;
   The one heart that beats within all breasts is mine.
   The world's happiness flows through me like wine,
Its million sorrows are my agonies.

Yet all its acts are only waves that pass
   Upon my surface; inly for ever still,
   Unborn I sit, timeless, intangible:
All things are shadows in my tranquil glass.

My vast transcendence holds the cosmic whirl;
I am hid in it as in the sea a pearl.

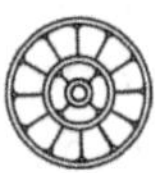

NOVEMBER 20, 1971

(Mother hands Satprem two notes.)

"We are at a moment of transition in the history of the earth. It is a moment only in terms of the eternity of time. But compared to human life this moment is long. Matter is in the process of changing to prepare for a new manifestation; but the human body is not sufficiently plastic and offers resistance. This is why the number of incomprehensible disorders and diseases is increasing and becoming a problem for medical science.

The remedy lies in union with the divine forces which are at work and in a confident and quiet receptivity that facilitates the process."

November 18, 1971

"Those who want to progress have an exceptional chance; because the transformation begins by opening the consciousness to the working of the new forces; and thus individuals have a unique and marvelous opportunity to open to the divine influence."

November 20, 1971

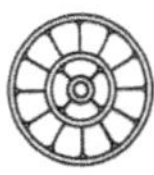

DECEMBER 25, 1971

This creation's goal is that Consciousness of the Infinite, the Eternal, which is omnipotent – Infinite, Eternal, Omnipotent (which our religions have called God: for us, with respect to life, it's the Divine) – Infinite and Eternal, All-Powerful ... outside of time: each individual particle possessing that Consciousness; each individual particle containing that same Consciousness.

Division created the world, and it is in division that the Eternal manifests.

Words are stupid, but that's how it is. I don't know if you follow.

(silence)

With, in addition (and not as a contradiction, but as a complement), the exact sense of what you are supposed to do – what you are supposed to be, what you are supposed to do and why you have been created. And all that TOGETHER ... OH!... *(Mother has a blissful smile)*

That gives both the reason and the goal of creation – both at once – and almost the method of development.

(silence)

Yes, it's like something that IS, that is as a whole and is successively projected on a screen. And yet it exists as a whole – and it is projected successively on a screen.

(Mother goes into contemplation)

I have the impression that I am on the way to discovering ... the illusion that must be destroyed so that physical life can be uninterrupted – discovering that death comes from a ... a distortion of consciousness. That's it.

It's this close, you know *(Mother makes a gesture as if she were about to grasp the secret)*.

And as I told you, sometimes I feel that the great number of years makes the work somewhat more difficult, but taken on the whole, it is a GREAT help – I understood that were I young, I could never have done what I am doing. And when I am in the true consciousness, the moment I am in the true consciousness, the number of years is nothing! – The body feels so young, so full of ... something else than young (for it, young is *immature* and ignorant, it's not that), it's ... you're in communion with "something" ... which changes according to the need.

Our language (or our consciousness) is ... inadequate. Later I'll be able to say.

Something IS HAPPENING – that's all I can say. *(Mother laughs)* Merry Christmas, mon petit!

Merry Christmas to you too.

The festival of Light....

COSMIC CONSCIOUSNESS

I have wrapped the wide world in my wider self
    And Time and Space my spirit's seeing are.
I am the god and demon, ghost and elf,
    I am the wind's speed and the blazing star.

All Nature is the nursling of my care,
    I am the struggle and the eternal rest;
The world's joy thrilling runs through me, I bear
    The sorrow of millions in my lonely breast.

I have learned a close identity with all,
    Yet am by nothing bound that I become;
Carrying in me the universe's call
    I mount to my imperishable home.

I pass beyond Time and life on measureless wings,
Yet still am one with born and unborn things.

MARCH 24, 1972

[Conversation with Sujata.]

For the first time, early this morning, I saw myself: my body. I don't know whether it's the supramental body or ... (what shall I say?) a transitional body, but I had a completely new body, in the sense that it was sexless: it was neither woman nor man.

It was very white. But that could be because I have white skin, I don't know.

It was very slender (*gesture*). Really lovely, a truly harmonious form.

That's the first time.

I hadn't the least idea, the faintest notion what it would look like, nothing, and I saw – I WAS like that, I had become like that. I thought Satprem should know, so he can note it down.

I don't know if I'll remember, that's why I am telling you. Because today is Friday and I won't see him till tomorrow. This way, I am sure I won't forget. You'll tell him, won't you?

Yes, Mother.

It's been hard.

Especially for food: it will be very different. I am BEGINNING to understand how it will work, but I don't know enough yet to describe it – I haven't had the experience, so I don't know.... Most probably, we will absorb things that don't need to be digested – there are some. But not food as such. For example, one idea these days is glucose (things of that sort). But I am not sure because I am just undergoing the experience. Once I have the vision of what to do, I'll do it.

Anyway, I wanted to tell you.

MARCH 25, 1972

[Regarding the conversation of March 24 about the new body.]

Yes, I WAS like that. It was me; I didn't look at myself in a mirror, I saw myself like this (*Mother bends her head to look at her body*), I was ... I just was like that.

That's the first time. It was around four in the morning, I think. And perfectly natural – I mean, I didn't look in a mirror, it felt perfectly natural. I only remember what I saw (*gesture from the chest to the waist*). I was covered only with veils, so I only saw.... What was very different was the torso, from the chest to the waist: it was neither male nor female.

But it was lovely, my form was extremely svelte and slim – slim but not thin. And the skin was very white, just like my skin. A lovely form. And no sex – you couldn't tell: neither male nor female. The sex had disappeared.

The same here (*Mother points to her chest*), all that was flat. I don't know how to explain it. There was an outline reminiscent of what is now, but with no forms (*Mother touches her chest*), not even as much as a man's. A very white skin, very smooth. Practically no abdomen to speak of. And no stomach. All that was slim.

I didn't pay any special attention, you see, because I was that: it felt perfectly natural to me. That's the first time it happened, it was the night before last; but last night I didn't see anything. That was the first and the last time so far.

But this form is in the subtle physical, isn't it?

It must be already like that in the subtle physical.

But how will it pass into the physical?

That's the question I don't know.... I don't know.
I don't know.
Also, clearly there was none of the complex digestion we have now, or the kind of elimination we have now. It didn't work that way.
But how? ... Food is already obviously very different and becoming more and more so – glucose, for instance, or substances that don't require an elaborate digestion. But how will the body itself change? ... That I don't know. I don't know.

You see, I didn't look to see how it worked, for it was completely natural to me, so I can't describe it in detail. Simply, it was neither a woman's body nor a man's – that much is certain. And the *outline* was fairly similar to that of a very young person. There was a faint suggestion of a human form *(Mother draws a form in the air):* with a shoulder and a waist. Just a hint of it.

I see it but.... I saw it exactly as you see yourself, I didn't even look at myself in the mirror. And I had a sort of veil, which I wore to cover myself.

It was my way of being (there was nothing surprising in it), my natural way of being.

That must be how it is in the subtle physical.

But what's mysterious is the transition from one to the other.

Yes – how?

But it's the same mystery as the transition from chimpanzee to man.

Oh, no, Mother! It's more colossal than that! It's more colossal for, after all, there isn't that much difference between a chimpanzee and a man.

But there wasn't such a difference in the appearance either *(Mother draws a form in the air):* there were shoulders, arms, legs, a body, a waist. Similar to ours. There was only....

Yes, but I mean the way a chimpanzee functions and the way a man functions are the same.

They are the same.

Well, yes! They digest the same, breathe the same.... Whereas here....

No, but here too there must have been breathing. The shoulders were strikingly broad *(gesture)*, in contrast.

That's important. But the chest was neither feminine nor even masculine: only reminiscent of it. And all that – stomach, abdomen and the rest – was simply an *outline*, a very slender and harmonious form, which certainly wasn't used for the purpose we now use our bodies.

The two different things – totally different – were procreation, which was no longer possible, and food. Though even our present food is manifestly not the same as that of chimpanzees or even the first humans; it's quite different. So now, it seems we have to find a food that doesn't require all this digesting.... Not exactly liquid, but not solid either. And there's also the question of the mouth – I don't know about that – and the teeth? Naturally, chewing should no longer be necessary, and therefore teeth wouldn't be either.... But there has to be something to replace them. I haven't the slightest idea what the face looked like. But it didn't seem too, too unlike what it is now.

What will change a great deal, of course – it had acquired a prominent role – is breathing. That being depended much on it.

Yes, he probably absorbs energies directly.

Yes. There will probably be intermediary beings who won't last, you see, just as there were intermediary beings between the chimpanzee and man.

But I don't know, something has to happen that has never before happened.

Yes.

(silence)

Sometimes I have a sort of feeling that the time of realization is very close.

Yes, but how?

Yes, how – we don't know.

Is this *(Mother points to her body)* going to change? It either has to change or else follow the old, ordinary pattern of coming undone and then being redone again.... I don't know. True, life can be greatly prolonged, there have been examples, but.... I don't know.
I don't know.

Several times I felt that instead of a transformation, there will be a concretization of the other body.

Ahh! ... But how?

We don't know the process either. But instead of this body becoming the other, the other body will take the place of this one.

Yes, but how?

How, I don't know.

(after a silence)
Yes, understandably, if the body I had two nights ago were to materialize.... But how? Do you want to meditate?

(Mother goes into contemplation)
We know nothing! It's amazing how we know NOTHING.

(Satprem prepares to leave, Sujata draws near to Mother)

(Sujata:) You know, Mother, in his poem "Transformation,
Sri Aurobindo's opening lines are:

"My breath runs in a subtle rhythmic stream;
It fills my members with a might divine:"

Breathing, yes, that's important. "A might"?

"Might," yes, Mother.

TRANSFORMATION

My breath runs in a subtle rhythmic stream;
   It fills my members with a might divine:
   I have drunk the Infinite like a giant's wine.
Time is my drama or my pageant dream.
Now are my illumined cells joy's flaming scheme
     And changed my thrilled and branching nerves to fine
     Channels of rapture opal and hyaline
For the influx of the Unknown and the Supreme.

I am no more a vassal of the flesh,
   A slave to Nature and her leaden rule;
     I am caught no more in the senses' narrow mesh.
My soul unhorizoned widens to measureless sight,
   My body is God's happy living tool,
     My spirit a vast sun of deathless light.

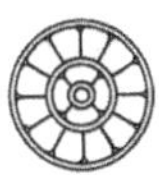

MARCH 30, 1972

Mother, your force is extremely active right now, you know.

Yes, I know. I know: when I am like now, I always see the Force – it isn't "my" force, it is the Divine Force. I try – I only try to be like this *(gesture like a channel)*. This body tries to be simply ... simply a transmitter, as transparent as possible, as impersonal as possible. So the Divine can do whatever He wants.

(silence)

It has become very transparent. For as soon as something is put before you, the action is done immediately.

(silence)

Yesterday, it was fifty-eight years since I came here for the first time. For fifty-eight years I have been working FOR THAT, for the body to be as transparent and immaterial as possible, so that it doesn't obstruct the descending Force.

Now – now it's the body itself, the body wants this with all its cells. That is its only purpose in life.

To try, to try to create on earth one completely transparent, translucent element that would let the force pass through without any distortion.

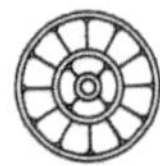

MAY 6, 1972

…Really, it's very simple: the whole creation must want nothing but the Divine, want nothing but to manifest the Divine; all its actions (including its so-called mistakes) are a means to make it inevitable for the whole creation to manifest the Divine – but not a "Divine" as man usually conceives of, with all kinds of limitations and restrictions: a TOTALITY of tremendous power and light.

Truly the Power is IN the world, a new and stupendous Power which has come into the world to manifest the divine Almightiness and make it "manifestable," so to say.

Through careful observation and attention, I have come to this conclusion: I have seen that what we call the "Supramental," for lack of a better word, is actually making the creation more susceptible to the higher Power, which we call "divine" because we … (it is divine compared to what we are, but …). It's something (*gesture of descent*

130

and pressure) that will make Matter more susceptible and responsive to the Force. How can I explain it? ... At present, whatever is invisible or imperceptible is unreal to us (I mean to human beings in general); we say that some things are "concrete" and others are not. But this Power, this Might, which is NOT MATERIAL, is becoming more concretely effective on earth than earthly material things. That's it.

And that is how the supramental beings will protect and defend themselves. In its appearance it won't be material but OVER MATTER its power will be greater than material things. Day by day, hour by hour this is getting truer and truer. The feeling that when this Force is guided by what we call the "Divine," it has POWER, a real power – the power to move Matter, you understand; it can cause a MATERIAL accident, or save you from a wholly material accident, it can cancel the consequences of an absolutely material event – it is stronger than Matter. This is the totally new and incomprehensible fact. But it ... *(fluttering gesture in the atmosphere)*, it creates a sort of panic in the ordinary human consciousness.

That's it. It seems that ... things are no longer what they were. There's really something new – things are NO LONGER what they were.

All our common sense, our human logic, our practical sense – collapsed, finished! No longer effective. No longer realistic. They are no longer relevant.

A new world, really.

(silence)

And in the body, whatever has trouble adjusting to this new Power creates difficulties, disorders and illnesses. Yet in a flash you sense that if you were totally receptive, you would become formidable. That's the sensation. That's more and more my sensation: that if the entire consciousness, the entire most material consciousness –

the most material – were receptive to this new Power ... one would become for-mi-dable.

(Mother closes her eyes)

But there is one essential condition: the ego's reign must come to an end. The ego is now the obstacle. The ego must be replaced by the divine consciousness – what personally I call divine consciousness. Sri Aurobindo called it "supramental," so we can call it supramental to avoid confusion, because as soon as you say "Divine," people start thinking of a "God," and that spoils everything. It isn't like that. Not like that, it is the descent of the supramental world *(Mother slowly lowers her fists)*, which is not mere imagination *(pointing above)*: it is an ABSOLUTELY material Power. But *(smilingly)* with no need for any material means.

A world is trying to be born into this world.

(silence)

On several occasions, my body felt a sort of new discomfort, an anxiety; and something, not exactly a voice but it became words in my consciousness, said, "Why are you afraid? This is the new consciousness." It happened several times. Then I understood.

(silence)

You see, what in terms of human common sense says, "This is impossible, it's never been before," that's what is finished. This idiocy is over. It's become a stupidity. Now we could say: it's possible BECAUSE it has never been before. This is the new world and this is the new consciousness and this is the new Power; it is possible, and it is, and will be more and more manifest BECAUSE it is the new world, because it has never been before.

It will be because it has never been before.

(silence)

It's lovely: it will be because it has never been before –
BECAUSE it has never been.

*(Mother looks up as if about to say something, then goes into
meditation)*

It is active – in you too. Not material and yet more
concrete than Matter!

Yes, almost crushing.

Crushing, yes, just so.... Oh, it's....
Whatever isn't receptive feels crushed, but all that is
receptive on the contrary feels a sort of ... extraordinary
expansion.

Yes. But that's what's so odd, there's both!

Yes, both together.

*You feel so expanded, as if everything in you would blow up,
but at the same time there's a sensation of being crushed ...*

Yes, but what feels crushed is what resists, what is
unreceptive. One has only to open oneself. Then it
becomes like a ... a for-mi-dable thing. Fabulous! It's our
centuries-old habits that resist and give us that feeling,
you know, but whatever can open up.... You feel as if you
were becoming larger and larger and larger.... Magnificent.
Oh, that's it! ...

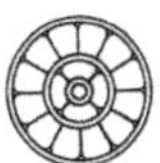

MAY 27, 1972

I really think the physical world is changing. People will
probably notice it only in a few hundred years, because it
takes a long time for it to become visible to the ordinary
consciousness. But the touch *(Mother feels the air between
her fingers)*, feels ... as if a different texture.

From time to time, something tells me, "Don't talk, don't talk!" I have to keep quiet otherwise people around me would think I am becoming deranged.

!!!

(long silence)

You say it isn't the way you see the physical world that's changing but the very quality of matter?

Yes, yes, it's not at all my own way of seeing – not at all.... I don't know.... But it's odd.

You see, I have at the same time (to speak in the old way), at the same time the CONCRETE experience of a tre-men-dous Power and of total impotence.

The old methods, the methods that even yesterday were effective and powerful, all seem nonexistent. Yet, side by side, when that Force comes, I concretely feel (and I have proof, a factual proof) that a simple expression of will, or even a simple vision of something is ... *(Mother lowers her hands)* all-powerful. Materially so. Some people on their deathbeds are returned to life; some healthy people, brrt, suddenly pass away – to that extent, you know. Circumstances that seemed inextricable find marvelous solutions – people themselves say it's miraculous. It's not miraculous to me, it's very simple: just like this *(Mother lowers a finger)*. But it's INDISPUTABLE. Indisputable and new in the world. No longer the old method, no longer a mental concentration or a mental vision, none of that *(Mother lowers a finger)*: a fact.

A fact.

I am myself still too much tied to ... [people's thoughts]. Thank God *(Mother sweeps her hand across her forehead)*, the mind is gone! Ah, you know, I am ... what an extraordinary blessing it is! But from the ordinary external standpoint, I seem to have become an utter imbecile.

!!!

It's good that I have someone like you near me who knows there's something else [than what they think].

Oh, indeed! [laughing] Indeed, there's "something else"!

And I feel such a force, you know.... When I rest, I don't sleep, I consciously enter that supramental activity, and.... Oh, mon petit! ... I see myself doing things with such a fabulous power! And there's no longer any ... you see, when I speak, I am forced to use "I," but it corresponds to nothing, it's ... it's the Consciousness, it's a consciousness. A consciousness that knows and has power. Yes, a CONSCIOUSNESS; not a person but a consciousness – a consciousness that knows and acts. And which uses this *(Mother points to her body)* to keep a contact with people.

Yes, that's it, it's not a person anymore – sometimes, you know *(laughing)*, I feel like a puppet *(gesture of dangling at the end of a string)* whose purpose is to enable contact with people. But the physical strength is like this *(wobbly gesture)....* I feel very strong – very strong, and almost nonexistent. Both extremes together, you understand.... I must really look stupid.

But there *(Mother stretches her arms upwards, then slowly extends them as if to embrace the universe)*, it's luminous, it's clear, it's strong, it's wide.... Physically, too. It is PHYSICAL, that's what is amazing! Before, I used to withdraw into an inner state of being (I know them all, I've experienced them, I've had a conscious life), but all that, all that is ... finished. Completely finished.... *(Smiling)* As if the physical world were becoming double.

Naturally, to the ordinary eye, I am still an old woman sitting in a chair and unable to move freely. Although at times, I suddenly feel that if I stood up, I could walk perfectly well.... But something tells me, "Patience, patience, patience ..." So I wait.

And there's a persistent idea *(hammering gesture)* that if I can reach, if my body can reach one hundred, it will become young again. It's very persistent, but doesn't come from me, it's like this *(hammering gesture from above),* so that I remain patient (although I am not impatient). Patience.

From now to one hundred is six years?

Yes, six years, Mother, it's not much.

But the body's capacities will change BEFORE its appearance changes – the appearance changes LAST, and I don't know, that never enters the picture.

What really matters is how the Consciousness can use this. It's not that I will become young again, it's not "young," it's another type of capacity that will emerge and use this body. Will it transform it? Or will it use it for another purpose? That I don't know.... I don't know. Strangely enough, only when you are here do I speak or think about these things, as if it were necessary for someone to know – otherwise, I never think about these things *(gesture of hands open).*

Sometimes I spend hours in contemplation doing a very, very active work. Sometimes there are a few minutes ... a few minutes of silence and contemplation ... that last hours. And they seem like a few minutes. That's how it is.

NOVEMBER 8, 1972

For a moment – just a few seconds – I had the supramental consciousness. It was so marvelous, mon petit! ... I understood that if we were to taste that now, we would no longer want to exist differently. We are in the process of ... *(gesture of kneading dough)* of changing laboriously. And the change, the process of change seems.... Yet you can grasp it in a kind of indifference (I don't know how to express it). But it doesn't last long. As a rule it's ... laborious. But that consciousness is so marvelous, you know! It's most interesting because there's a sort of EXTREME activity within complete peace. But it lasted only a few seconds.

(silence hands turned upwards)

And you?

Is it a total consciousness?

It's fabulous! Like a harmonization of all opposites. Yes, a total, fantastic activity together with ... perfect peace. But these are mere words.

(silence)

Is this consciousness material?

The action is a material one – but not done in the same way, of course.

(silence)

What helps make the contact with "that"? ... What exactly makes you go across there or be there?

I don't know because I am constantly – my WHOLE consciousness, including that of the body, is always turned to the ... *(gesture of offering)* to what it feels as the Divine. And without "trying," you follow?

Yes. Yes.

(Mother plunges in)

A last and mightiest transformation came.
His soul was all in front like a great sea
·Flooding the mind and body with its waves;
His being, spread to embrace the universe,
United the within and the without
To make of life a cosmic harmony,
An empire of the immanent Divine.
In this tremendous universality
Not only his soul-nature and mind-sense
Included every soul and mind in his,
But even the life of flesh and nerve was changed
And grew one flesh and nerve with all that lives;
He felt the joy of others as his joy,
He bore the grief of others as his grief;
His universal sympathy upbore,
Immense like ocean, the creation's load
As earth upbears all beings' sacrifice,
Thrilled with the hidden Transcendent's joy and peace.
There was no more division's endless scroll;
One grew the Spirit's secret unity,
All Nature felt again the single bliss.
There was no cleavage between soul and soul,
There was no barrier between world and God.
Overpowered were form and memory's limiting line;
The covering mind was seized and torn apart;
It was dissolved and now no more could be,
The one Consciousness that made the world was seen;
All now was luminosity and force.
Abolished in its last thin fainting trace
The circle of the little self was gone;
The separate being could no more be felt;

It disappeared and knew itself no more,
Lost in the spirit's wide identity.
His nature grew a movement of the All,
Exploring itself to find that all was He,
His soul was a delegation of the All
That turned from itself to join the one Supreme.

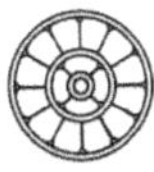

DECEMBER 20, 1972

I had a question about Sri Aurobindo. I was wondering what stage he had reached when he left – what stage in the transformation? For instance, what difference is there between the work you are doing now and what he was doing at the time?

He had accumulated a great deal of supramental force in his body, and as soon as he left he.... He was on his bed, you see, and I was standing beside him, and all the supramental force that was in him passed quite concretely from his body into mine – so concretely that I thought it was visible. I could feel the friction of the passage. It was extraordinary – extraordinary! It was an extraordinary experience. It went on for a long, long time like this *(gesture of the Force passing into Mother's body)*. I was standing beside his bed, and it passed into me.

Almost physical – it was a physical sensation. It lasted a long time.

That's all I know.

DECEMBER 30, 1972

Things have taken an extreme form. There's a sort of lifting of the whole atmosphere towards an almost ... inconceivable splendor, but at the same time, there's a feeling that one can ... die any moment – not "die," but the body could dissolve. Both things together make up a consciousness in which... *(Mother shakes her head)* all past experiences seem puerile, childish, unconscious. And this ... is stupendous and wonderful.

But the body, the body has a single prayer – always the same:

Make me worthy of knowing You
Make me worthy of serving You
Make me worthy of being You
There.

I can barely eat anymore, and I am not hungry. I feel a growing strength in me ... but new in quality ... in silence and contemplation.

Nothing is impossible *(Mother opens her hands upward)*.

(silence)

So if you don't have any questions to ask.... If you want silence ... conscious silence ...?

But am I making the right movement, I'm not sure?

Well, when you want to come into contact with the Divine, what movement do you make?

I place myself at your feet.

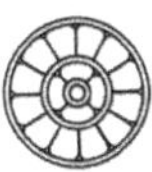

I can't talk, it doesn't come out clearly.

But that's not true! It does! It comes out very well.

If you have a question, we can try.

I don't know, whenever I try to come into contact with that Consciousness, I always sense a sort of luminous immensity, as you say....

Yes.

But I feel it's stationary, you see; I am in it and could stay in it forever, but....

Exactly. That's my own sensation too.

But is it enough to let That permeate one? Isn't there anything else to be done?

Yes, I think so. I think it's the only thing to do. Personally I keep repeating, "What You will, what You will, what You will.... Let it be as You will, may I do as You will, may I be conscious of what You will."

And also: "Without You, it's death; with You, it's life." By "death," I don't mean physical death – it might happen, it might be that if I lost the contact now, it would be the end – but that's impossible! I feel that ... I AM THAT – With some resistances the present consciousness may still have, that's all.

And when I see somebody ... (*Mother opens her hands as if she were offering that person to the Light*), regardless of who it is: like this (*same gesture*).

(silence)

It's funny, I constantly feel like a little baby curled up – curled up in ... (what term to use?) an *all-embracing* divine Consciousness.

TRANCE OF WAITING

Lone on my summits of calm I have brooded with voices
around me,
    Murmurs of silence that steep mind in a luminous sleep,
Whispers from things beyond thought in the Secrecy flame
white for ever,
    Unscanned heights that reply seek from the inconscient
    deep.
Distant below me the ocean of life with its passionate surges
    Pales like a pool that is stirred by the wings of a
    shadowy bird.
Thought has flown back from its wheelings and stoopings,
the nerve-beat of living
    Stills my spirit at peace bathes in a mighty release.
Wisdom supernal looks down on me, Knowledge mind
cannot measure;
    Light that no vision can render garments the silence
    with splendour.
Filled with a rapturous Presence the crowded spaces of being
    Tremble with the Fire that knows, thrill with the
    might of repose.
Earth is now girdled with trance and Heaven is put round
her for vesture.
    Wings that are brilliant with fate sleep at Eternity's gate.
Time waits, vacant, the Lightning that kindles, the Word
that transfigures;
    Space is a stillness of God building his earthly abode.
All waits hushed for the fiat to come and the tread
of the Eternal;
    Passion of a bliss yet to be sweeps from Infinity's sea.

References

The passages in this book have been selected from the following publications:

Collected Works of Sri Aurobindo: (CWSA).

Collected Works of The Mother: (CWM).

Mother's Agenda: (MA).

1   CWSA, Vol. 2, p. 595
    CWSA, Vol. 34, ed., 2005, p. 369

2   CWSA, Vol. 34, ed., 2005, p. 693
    CWSA, Vol. 21, ed., 2005, p. 1

3   CWSA, Vol. 21, ed., 2005, p. 47
    CWSA, Vol. 34, ed., 2005, p. 652
    CWSA, Vol. 21, ed., 2005, p. 5

4   CWSA, Vol. 34, ed., 2005, p. 648

5   CWM, Vol. 5, 2nd ed., p. 178

6   CWSA, Vol. 22, ed., 2005, p. 1059

7   CWSA, Vol. 34, ed., 2005, p. 704

8   CWSA, Vol. 13, ed., 1998, p. 531

9   CWSA, Vol. 2, p. 595
    CWSA, Vol. 22, ed., 2005, p. 1090

10 CWSA, Vol. 21, ed., 2005, p. 141

11 CWSA, Vol. 13, ed., 1998, p. 533

12 CWSA, Vol. 34, ed., 2005, p. 707
    CWSA, Vol. 22, ed., 2005, p. 997

13 CWSA, Vol. 13, ed., 1998, p. 534

14 CWSA, Vol. 2, p. 594
    CWSA, Vol. 13, ed., 1998, p. 563

15 CWM, Vol. 5, 2nd ed., p. 141

16 CWSA, Vol. 33, ed., 2005, p. 343

17 CWSA, Vol. 13, ed., 1998, p. 561
    CWM, Vol. 5, 2nd ed., p. 180

18 CWSA, Vol. 2, p. 578

19 MA, Vol. 1, p. 35

21 CWSA, Vol. 33, ed., 2005, p. 343
    MA, Vol. 1, p. 112

23 CWM, Vol. 8, 2nd ed., p. 188
    CWM, Vol. 8, 2nd ed., p. 190

24 CWM, Vol. 9, 2nd ed., p. 271

30 MA, Vol. 2, p. 20

32 CWSA, Vol. 2, p. 601
    MA, Vol. 2, p. 375

34 MA, Vol. 3, p. 39

36 MA, Vol. 3, p. 131

38 CWSA, Vol. 33, ed., 2005, p. 322

39 MA, Vol. 3, p. 137

42 CWSA, Vol. 22, ed., 2005, p. 723
    MA, Vol. 3, p. 144

45 MA, Vol. 4, p. 55
    CWSA, Vol. 13, ed., 1998, p. 533

46 MA, Vol. 5, p. 73

47 MA, Vol. 6, p. 70

48 MA, Vol. 6, p. 96
    MA, Vol. 6, p. 185

49 MA, Vol. 6, p. 224

52 CWSA, Vol. 13, ed., 1996, p. 558

53 MA, Vol. 6, p. 228
    MA, Vol. 7, p. 217

60 MA, Vol. 7, p. 243

62 CWSA, Vol. 2, p. 602
    MA, Vol. 8, p. 30

64 MA, Vol. 8, p. 213

66 MA, Vol. 8, p. 308

67 MA, Vol. 8, p. 375

78 CWSA, Vol. 13, ed., 1998, p. 558

79 MA, Vol. 9, p. 182

81 CWSA, Vol. 21, ed., 2005, p. 111

82 MA, Vol. 9, p. 203
    MA, Vol. 9, p. 210

83 MA, Vol. 9, p. 266

84 CWSA, Vol. 13, ed., 1998, p. 571

85 MA, Vol. 9, p. 332

87 MA, Vol. 9, p. 349

89 MA, Vol. 10, p. 18

93 CWSA, Vol. 33, ed., 2005, p. 289

94 MA, Vol. 10, p. 26

95 MA, Vol. 10, p. 28

96 MA, Vol. 10, p. 29

99 MA, Vol. 10, p. 32

100 MA, Vol. 10, p. 63

103 CWSA, Vol. 33, ed., 2005, p. 322

104 MA, Vol. 10, p. 425

105 MA, Vol. 10, p. 438
    CWSA, Vol. 34, ed., 2005, p. 662

106 MA, Vol. 10, p. 463

107 MA, Vol. 11, p. 129

109 MA, Vol. 11, p. 261

110 MA, Vol. 11, p. 277

114 MA, Vol. 11, p. 245

116 MA, Vol. 12, p. 300

120 CWSA, Vol. 2, p. 601
    MA, Vol. 12, p. 303

121 MA, Vol. 12, p. 347

123 CWSA, Vol. 2, p. 603
    MA, Vol. 13, p. 96

124 MA, Vol. 13, p. 98

129 CWSA, Vol. 2, p. 561
    MA, Vol. 13, p. 118

130 MA, Vol. 13, p. 177

133 MA, Vol. 13, p. 191

136 MA, Vol. 13, p. 308

138 CWSA, Vol. 33, ed., 2005, p. 318

139 MA, Vol. 13, p. 326

140 MA, Vol. 13, p. 332

141 MA, Vol. 13, p. 374

143 CWSA, Vol. 2, p. 573

Other books published by PRISMA

Antithesis of Yoga
by Jocelyn

Finding the Psychic Being
by Loretta Shartsis

The Mother on Japan
by The Mother

The Teachings of Flowers
(The Life and Work of the Mother of the
Sri Aurobindo Ashram)
by Loretta Shartsis

Death doesn't exist
The Mother on Death, Sri Aurobindo on Rebirth
by The Mother

Passage to More than India
by Dick Batstone

The Supramental Transformation
by Loretta Shartsis

Children of Change: A Spiritual Pilgrimage
by Amrit

Memories of Auroville - told by early Aurovilians
by Janet Fearn

Bougainvilleas PROTECTION
by Narad (Richard Eggenberger), Nilisha Mehta

The Mother's Yoga - 1956-1973 (Vol. 1, 1956-1967)
by Loretta Shartsis

The Mother's Yoga - 1956-1973 (Vol. 2, 1968-1973)
by Loretta Shartsis

Crossroad The New Humanity
by Paulette Hadnagy

www.ingramcontent.com/pod-product-compliance
Lightning Source LLC
Chambersburg PA
CBHW071751150726
47998CB00005B/1887